NEVER CAST OUT

HOW THE GOSPEL PUTS AN END
TO THE STORY OF SHAME

NEVER CAST OUT

Jasmine L. Holmes

B&H
PUBLISHING
BRENTWOOD, TENNESSEE

To the faithful Black women in my life who consistently interrupt the message of shame. I see you.

ACKNOWLEDGMENTS

Phillip, it's the same old song: I would never be able to write a single word without your support. You are a gift.

Abena, Portia, Bethny, Charaia, you are the Black girls this book is dedicated to. You have all held my hand through so much of the shame that threatens to pull me under.

Denine Blevins, our conversation about fig leaves was foundational in changing the way I thought about shame and the garden. I am so grateful for you and the work you do through Parakaleo.

Ashley, this book would not be possible without you. From our very first meeting, I've approached this project with fear and trembling, and your confidence and guidance have been an anchor.

CONTENTS

Introduction

Writing this book has been a constant battle with shame. Which, of course, makes sense, given its topic. It's like that old saying about not asking God for patience—because as soon as you ask him, he'll start giving you all kinds of opportunities to grow your patience through trials. Asking God to tackle the shame in my life was like inviting my good friend shame for an extended stay.

There are so many ways that we could approach a book about shame. I have read so much on shame from therapists, researchers, and academics. I have been greatly helped by those volumes, and there is a list of them that I could commend to you.

This is not one of those books.

I am not a therapist talking to you about what shame does to the brain. I am not a researcher talking about how shame cripples so many areas of our lives. I am not an academic discussing the intricacies of shame's presence in the Old and New Testaments.

So here is who I am:

I am a Christian and a pastor's kid who is now raising children in that same faith.

I am a millennial who is watching her peers undergo deconstruction as they grapple with that faith.

I am a woman and a wife who is trying to find her place in a society that seems so much easier to navigate as a man.

I am a Black woman who has spent her entire life in majority-white evangelical contexts, trying to contextualize experiences for which language is still being developed.

Sometimes shame is hoisted on our shoulders in one big traumatic event, like a big boulder. Other times it adds weight to our shoulders incrementally, one pebble at a time, to where we barely notice the escalating weight. In this book I'm going to give you examples of the latter, because I'm not a trauma therapist, rather, I'm a fellow believer who has had to learn the skill of recognizing incremental doses of shame that have not been met with the gospel. Said another way, if you start reading and you begin to think: *Wow, these seem like trivial examples compared to the heavy things I've had to bear when it comes to shame,* you'd be right. My goal, though, isn't to dodge the "real problems," rather, to help you see shame in the places you typically miss it. In short, I'm staying in my lane, and ultimately, I'm simply trying to paint in broad brushstrokes when it comes to the way the gospel speaks to shame, because it's a part of the gospel I didn't have eyes to see for far too long. I want to help you see it, too, especially in those small and seemingly insignificant experiences, and where you've been carrying it, I want the gospel to send it packing.

I have been a Christian since I was six years old, which means I've known Jesus pretty much all my life. But I did not know until just recently that Jesus *despised* the shame that so often had me bound.

In my mind, shame was a tool that Jesus was using to whip me into shape, or a by-product of the fact that I just needed to be trying harder. Shame was something that belonged in my Christian walk as a reminder not to step out of line. I viewed shame as a frenemy of sorts—it tortured me, yes, but, surely, it sanctified me as well.

I must have read Hebrews 12:1–2 so many times before, but it wasn't until I started staring shame in the face that some of the words jumped out at me anew:

> . . . let us run with endurance the race that is set
> before us, fixing our eyes on Jesus, the author and
> perfecter of faith, who for the joy set before Him
> endured the cross, **despising the shame**, and has
> sat down at the right hand of the throne of God.
> (NASB 1995)

Despising shame.

This passage is talking about the specific humiliation that came with being hung on a cross, of course, but it also shows us Jesus's posture toward the power shame holds over humans in general. If he hated—*despised*—the most severe form of humiliation and degradation this world can throw at a person, how must he feel about all the smaller forms of it?

This idea that Jesus wasn't the author of the shame hanging over my life like a guillotine? That was news to me. And maybe it's news to you too. Maybe the idea that Jesus has not called us to shame, but to full-hearted confidence in him, rings dissonant in your ears.

I've been there.

Wherever you find yourself in life—whether you relate to any area of identity I've outlined, or you're on a different trajectory altogether—I want you to imagine that this book is an invitation to sit at the table next to me. I'm not at the head, but neither is shame. Instead, we turn toward the One who sets a table for us in the presence of our enemies (Ps. 23:5). We sit at the table with the One who speaks words of life into the raging seas. We sit next to the One who put shame to its rightful death.

I imagine a wide variety of responses to that proclamation. Maybe you're on one side of the spectrum, saying, *Heck yes! Shame is a thief and I am tired of having my joy stolen!* Maybe you're on the other side, rolling your eyes and saying, *Oh, no. Here comes another self-help book that tells me I'm a perfect little butterfly who has nothing to change.* Maybe your response is somewhere in between.

Wherever you land in your first-blush response to shame, this book is an invitation to dig deeper. It's an invitation to explore the story of the birth of shame in the garden, its eventual death on the cross at Calvary, and how we wrestle with its ghost until Jesus comes again. In part 1, we'll talk about where shame comes from, the lies it tells us, and the lousy, exhausting, and fruitless ways we try to remove it from our lives. In short, it gives you a broad look at the problem. In part 2, we'll talk about the truth the gospel teaches us in the face of that problem, and how Jesus offers us a far better solution. And in part 3, we'll talk about how to apply that gospel truth when we sense shame coming to haunt us in our daily experience, through the power of a few specific sources of grace in our lives.

This book is not a comprehensive examination of shame/honor culture, or a contrast of notions of shame around the world. It is written from a very particular perspective—one I hope will encourage people who relate to the struggles shared herein. It will not be exhaustive, because the beautiful thing about the vast body of Christ is that innumerable perspectives exist to meet each and every one of us where we are in our walk with Jesus.

It would be so easy for me to continue to focus on all that this book is *not*—all of the places where it's just not enough. It just scratches the surface in so many ways, as so many books do. But rather than looking at this book like the be-all to end-all, I want you to look at it like the first step in a lifelong journey of grappling with this big emotion. It's the faintest outline of the picture you're painting of what your life could be if you truly believed the soul-deep truth that we serve a God who will **never cast us out** (John 6:37). A God who sees all of the areas where we struggle with shame, looks at them more deeply and intimately than we could ever imagine, and whispers, "Mine."

Always.

Maybe this is your very first step in the journey of believing those words. Maybe it's meeting you halfway through your journey, or closer to the other side, even, than I am. But we're all headed to the same place: deeper assurance in the matchless love of Jesus, who has covered our shame.

Let's get started.

PART 1

The Beginning of Shame

CHAPTER 1

Shoddy Fig Leaves That Can't Cover You

My very first memory is one of euphoric happiness. Or at least it started that way.

I was almost three years old. My mom was pregnant with my younger brother. We were sitting in her bedroom, Mommy on the floor, me on the edge of her bed, my hair box open next to me. For the uninitiated, the hair box was full of everything my mom needed to do my hair before day care every morning. Through the wonderous eyes of a three-year-old, it was chock-full of treasures: hair ties, baubles, and clips in a rainbow of colors.

Every day after school, Mommy sat on the floor in front of her bed and let me play in her hair. I would tie it into pigtails, clip in various hair accessories, and admire my artwork while she dozed in front of the evening news. I remember my excitement at waking her up to show her the beautiful styles I came up with, little legs kicking off the edge of the bed with unhampered enthusiasm.

My mom would wake up and ooh and aah over my skill. Sometimes, my dad would come home and join in the wonderment. My elaborate hair sculptures garnered the praise that any three-year-old yearns to hear from her parents. It made me feel like a big girl, doing Mommy's hair just like Mommy did mine every morning, and doing it in a way that pleased her.

On this day, I was feeling particularly creative. I dug past my normal comb, brush, and hair tie fare to the jar of pomade my mom used to pull my curly hair back into immaculate ponytails. I sheepishly held the jar over my mother's shoulder, and she cast a sleepy eye in my direction and shook her head. She said something like, "You don't need to use that, Jasmine."

That moment was the very first time I remember *shame*. That feeling of exposure and embarrassment. The lovely work of art I had planned was vetoed outright. With a simple *no*, I felt a cascade of . . . *bad feeling*. I felt the *no* in my marrow—it made me feel silly for bringing childish fancy into our very *big girl game* of hair salon. An activity that had been an intimate moment with "just us girls" before my brother came had turned into a (very gentle) reprimand that reminded me that I was still just a little girl, and not the boundless artist I had heretofore imagined.

It would be years until I realized that this feeling had a name: shame.

It would be even longer before I realized that this feeling would be a near-constant companion for the rest of my life.

It cropped up the first time I told a boy I liked him, and he rejected me outright. Came again when I failed my very first test. Haunted me as I stayed up night after night replaying social interactions that had gone wrong.

Shame is often associated with wrongdoing, but the older I got, the more I realized that I didn't have to sin to feel shame. Toddler-Jasmine wasn't *sinning* by wanting to use pomade . . . she just ran into a boundary that made her feel . . . *off.*

That shame grew old with me. It followed me down the aisle and into my marriage, perching watchfully in my first home and pointing out the dishes in the sink—the dust on the floorboards—the unmade bed.

It lurked in the room where I first found out that I'd had a miscarriage. I was *ashamed* that my body couldn't do something that seemed so simple for so many other women: carry a baby to term.

And when I did carry my baby to term, it buffeted me with all of the "shoulds" of early motherhood: baby *should* have a schedule, or mama *should* follow baby's lead . . . baby *should* only be nursing, or mama *should* just stop trying to force it and move on to formula . . . baby *should* always have mama's full attention, every waking moment of every day, but mama *should* not dote on baby too much or baby will be spoiled.

There were shameful shoulds at home . . . shameful shoulds at work . . . shameful shoulds in marriage . . . shameful shoulds in friendships. Sometimes they came when I did something wrong—snapped at my husband, grew impatient with my baby, sinned against a friend. But often, they came when I hadn't necessarily done something wrong, so much as shown the frailty of my humanity: been too tired to make up my bed after being awake all night with my baby, not had dinner ready when my husband got home because nursing my baby was a full-time job, or fallen off the face of the earth in my most treasured relationships because I was consumed with learning how to be a mother.

Each time, that feeling was the same: humiliation . . . alienation . . . the urge to hide.

Womanhood and Shame

At the time of writing this sentence, I am heavily pregnant with my third child. My middle boy is almost the exact same age I was on that day when Mommy let me play in her hair. Now, I can imagine my mother's perinatal exhaustion after a long day of work. I can feel the heavy limbs that loaded me into the car after day care, brought me home, and sat me on the edge of the bed with a hair box to keep me occupied until Daddy came home. Those little creations allowed her to doze after the exhaustion of teaching a classroom full of pupils while carting a melon-sized baby along inside of her.

But if I told my middle boy *no*, he likely would have just kicked his feet, shrugged, and redirected himself without my toddler ennui. My oldest, however, would have taken it to heart just like his mama, crumpling inwardly as the *no* signaled, not just a mother's loving boundary, but the *wrongness* of a choice that I had almost made.

I know because I've watched that exact feeling float across his face—the crestfallen crumpling of *shame*.

I have three boys, and I know at least one of them will be able to relate to the shame-spirals of a sensitive heart. My focus on women in this book, then, is not meant to imply that men don't *also* suffer with shame; it is, rather, to hone in on the unique aspects of female shame in our current societal climate and evangelical church context.

The dictionary defines *shame* as "a painful feeling of humili-ation or distress caused by the consciousness of wrong or foolish behavior." Its synonyms include *humiliation, mortification,* and *loss of face.*[1]

My dramatic flair—also a leftover from my toddler person-ality—prefers a quote often attributed to philosopher Jean-Paul Sartre: "Shame is a hemorrhage of the soul."[2]

That first prick of shame began when I was a small child, and the wound has been hemorrhaging ever since.

Shame has always been a background noise in my life—a low and persistent hum, a companion who is more frenemy than friend. But as I grew into womanhood, that low hum became a *din.* So many of the messages that I imbibed about what it meant to be a woman of God were laced with *shame* and *should.*

From "you *should* be married by now" to "you *should* be having children by now" to "you *should* have your career all figured out by now" or "you *should* only make a career of your children" . . . the cacophony blares in my ears.

Or . . . it used to blare. These days, I've dialed it back down to the manageable hum. And sometimes, on a good day . . . it goes quiet altogether.

Soul Awakening and Shame Awakening

But where did shame *start?*

Not for me, but for the world itself? Where did this universal and crushing emotion come from? Does the world, like me, have a first memory of shame?

Indeed, it does.

Like my first introduction to the feeling, it all started with beauty. And it all started at the very beginning.

Genesis is the book of beginnings. The God of the universe decides to begin the course of human history by breathing life, not just into the lungs of the first man in all of creation, but by breathing life into creation itself.

Even now, he invites mankind into the story he has chosen to weave for them before the dawn of time.

Adam begins the lineage of humankind, handmade by God in his image. The entirety of creation tells of God's glory—the birds of the air, the beasts of the field, even the rocks proclaim his marvelous handiwork.

But mankind proclaims God's glory in a different way—through the stewardship of all that God has created, through the fulfillment of his command to "fill the earth, and subdue it" (and through the Great Commission that God's Son has commanded of believers).

In the beginning, God created Adam and Eve in his very own image (Gen. 1:26–27) and he gave mankind a unique purpose:

> "Be fruitful, multiply, fill the earth, and sub-
> due it. Rule the fish of the sea, the birds of the
> sky, and every creature that crawls on the earth."
> (Gen. 1:28)

That purpose was then followed by abundance and generosity:

> "Look, I have given you every seed-bearing plant
> on the surface of the entire earth and every tree
> whose fruit contains seed. This will be food for
> you, for all the wildlife of the earth, for every bird

of the sky, and for every creature that crawls on
the earth—everything having the breath of life
in it—I have given every green plant for food."
(Gen. 1:29–30)

And that abundance was followed with a boundary:

"You are free to eat from any tree of the garden,
but you must not eat from the tree of the knowledge of good and evil, for on the day you eat from
it, you will certainly die." (Gen. 2:16–17)

In these few verses, we have all the ingredients for a soul-awak-
ening: life, calling, and limitations.

First, we have **life**: in Genesis 1, God is about the business of
creating something out of nothing. He takes the void and shapes it
into vegetation, sky, sea, and animals . . . all culminating in mankind, the crowning glory of his creation. He made the body and
soul of Adam and the body and soul of Eve—and then he gave
them a purpose: to subdue and to cultivate.

Our **callings**, then, are grounded first and foremost in our
servanthood to the One who has made us in his image. Any talk
of who we are must be rooted in whose we are. Our God is the
creator of the world, and we were made to inhabit that world, to
steward that world, to explore that world, and to proclaim his glorious name throughout that world.

And throughout time and history, we have done that in so
many ways. We have investigated the world we live in, pioneer-
ing scientific advances in our thirst to know more about everything from the tiniest cell in the human body to the biggest planet
in our solar system. We have mimicked our Creator by inventing

everything from the very first wheel to the very first hoverboard. We have multiplied and filled the earth with myriad people groups of every tribe, tongue, and nation, and we have set our minds to bridging the gaps between every tribe, tongue, and nation by making the Bible available in 670 languages.

We have gone to great, jaw-dropping lengths to explore the world that God has made. It is surreal to remember that the moon David surveyed in the Psalms has been tread upon and those stars he marveled at have begun to be numbered. We have gone to the ends of the earth to proclaim the good news: what started as a small movement of Jews and Gentiles in Rome has literally spread across the globe, right to where I'm writing you from Mississippi.

We image-bearers cannot help but follow the path that our Creator has set out for us. Even when we live lives of utter rejection to part of our calling (proclaiming his name), our thirst for knowledge, our bent for creativity, and our marveling at the world he has made screams that we were made in the image of someone bigger.

It screams that we are constantly searching for the heart of our identity, that we yearn to be identified with something—someone—beyond what we can see. We mimic our Creator whether we acknowledge him or not. We seek him out whether we do so knowingly, unknowingly, or begrudgingly. And there is evidence of him all over the creation that he breathed life into. There is evidence of him all over us.

But there are also **limitations**. Those limits define the boundaries of our existence. And those limitations are what gave birth to the very first moment of shame.

God created Adam and Eve in his own image, perfectly crafted to commune with him for all eternity. But, of course, they didn't stay that way. Just a short time after God placed Adam and Eve in the garden and laid out their purpose in creation, that purpose was tragically derailed by something called *the fall*. That term sounds just like it's supposed to. What it means is this: the first two sinless human beings ever created were walking uprightly—with both God and with each other. And then . . . well . . . they fell down.

You know the story. Eve, deceived by the serpent, disobeyed God's first law: "You must not eat from the tree of the knowledge of good and evil" (Gen. 2:17). Though she clearly knew this limitation, she ate the fruit of this tree anyway and gave the fruit to Adam. And ever since then, the children of Adam, deceived by the sinfulness of their own flesh, have disobeyed God's law.

Entire commentaries could (and have) been written on just the first three chapters of the Book of Beginnings, but I want to focus on what happened directly *before* and directly *after* Adam and Eve disobeyed God. Here's the state of affairs before they disobeyed:

> Both the man and his wife were **naked, yet felt no shame**. (Gen. 2:25)

Now, here's the state of things right after they disobeyed:

> The woman saw that the tree was good for food and delightful to look at, and that it was desirable for obtaining wisdom. So she took some of its fruit and ate it; she also gave some to her husband, who was with her, and he ate it. Then the eyes of

both of them were opened, and they **knew they were naked**; so they sewed fig leaves together and **made coverings for themselves**.

The man and his wife heard the sound of the Lord God walking in the garden at the time of the evening breeze, and **they hid from the Lord God** among the trees of the garden. So the Lord God called out to the man and said to him, "Where are you?"

And he said, "I heard you in the garden, and I was afraid because **I was naked, so I hid**." (Gen. 3:6–10)

Do you see the change? Before disobedience, Adam and Eve were naked, but they didn't know they were. They didn't feel exposed. There was nothing embarrassing about their existence to feel exposed *about*. Why would they be embarrassed? They were the only two humans on earth, and they belonged to each other completely as husband and wife. The only other being who saw them unclothed was their Creator. And so "they felt no shame." That's the picture of humanity before God when sin isn't part of the equation: *no shame*.

And then, after disobedience, they suddenly "knew" they were naked. They felt exposed for the first time in their entire lives. Embarrassed. In the wrong. Instead of "no shame," what do we see? They hid.

And somewhere between that moment of disobedience and the moment of hiding, *guilt* and *shame* were born. But they aren't the same.

Unlike the nebulous feeling of shame, which can float into our lives for all manner of reasons (some legitimate, some not), the state of someone's guilt is related to a specific wrongdoing: "the fact of having committed a specified or implied offense or crime."[3]

Adam and Eve were guilty the moment they disobeyed God's boundary about the fruit, whether they felt badly about it or not. Their guilt could be proven in a court of law: God said not to do x and you directly disobeyed him by doing x. There was proof, both in the eating of the fruit, and in the knowledge that came as a result. In short, guilt is a state of being, regardless of feelings. You either *are* guilty, or you're *not*.

Contrast this with shame, which, as we see in the passage above, is primarily an emotion and not a state of being. *Shame is feeling, not fact.* (Notice that Genesis 2:25 says they *felt* no shame.) The fact was that Adam and Eve had sinned. The feeling was the awareness of their nakedness—and their nakedness was symbolic of their shame. Where they once had God's approval wrapped around every bit of their existence, totally covering them, now they are exposed, and they *feel* that exposure. Said another way, shame was the emotional aftermath of their guilty state before God. They were guilty, now relationally exposed instead of covered, and so they felt shame.

And so what do they do with such a feeling? Adam and Eve acted quickly and foolishly, hiding themselves from the God of the universe in the garden that he himself had created. They sewed fig leaves together to cover their nakedness and waited in fear for the coming of their Lord.

Shame Isolates

Adam and Eve were discovering a truth that would echo throughout human existence on earth: Shame hides. It isolates.

Think of the illogic of Adam and Eve's decision. They have been hand-molded by a loving Father who has given them *every good thing*. Yes, they have disobeyed him and breached the one boundary he has given them—they are guilty. But rather than throw themselves upon the mercy of a God whom they *know* is good (everything about their existence has proven this about him), they hide.

And not only do they hide . . . they hide badly. They hide themselves in the garden of his creation and cover their nakedness with material that could float away at the provocation of one stiff breeze.

Look back at the passage and notice how God pulls them out of their isolation. He asks a question to which he, of course, already knows the answer: "Where are you?" (Gen. 3:9).

As we heard before, Adam answers: "I heard you in the garden, and I was afraid because I was naked, so I hid" (Gen. 3:10).

Here, also, we see the birth of fear. Adam and Eve had never had a reason to be afraid of God. He had not shown them his wrath—they had only seen his love. He had not shown his capacity for destruction—they had only seen him as Creator. He had not shown them the meaning of the word *consequence* . . . but they knew they were worthy of one.

Again, God asks a question to which he already knows the answer: "Who told you that you were naked? Did you eat from the tree that I commanded you not to eat from?" (Gen. 3:11).

In his mercy, God gives them an opportunity to simply be honest about what happened and confess their guilt. Yet, in their shame, they pass blame—Adam to Eve, and then Eve to the serpent. Rather than stand with the woman whom he proudly proclaimed as bone of his bone and flesh of his flesh, Adam distances himself both from God (in hiding) and from her (in blaming). Rather than throw herself on the mercy of the God who created her, Eve blames the serpent for her wrongdoing.

What was once a beautiful connection between God and humankind has been fractured by guilt, yes—by sin and wrongdoing—and, by *shame*—the compounding of the emotional impulse to hide wrongdoing for fear of embarrassment.

As Adam fears, all three of them—Adam, Eve, and serpent—receive consequences. But even in the words of the consequence itself, God bridges the chasm of isolation that shame has created when he tells the serpent:

> "And I will put enmity
> between you and the woman,
> and between your offspring and hers;
> he will crush your head,
> and you will strike his heel."
> (Gen. 3:15 NIV)

In those five lines, God promises to set right everything that the first sin has destroyed. He promises that someone is coming—someone who will eventually be born from this woman's bloodline. And God promises the serpent that this specific "someone" born of Eve has a mission—he will crush the head of the serpent. *You might try to strike his heel, serpent, and you'll think you're doing him damage, but this coming Son of Eve will demolish you—and all the effects of what you've done—once and for all.* Those of us on the other side of the New Testament have an idea of who this "someone" is. We have a guess at who would sacrifice himself for the guilt brought onto mankind through Adam and Eve's sin. But at this moment in the story, the point is that immediately after their disobedience, God is kind and provisional: instead of leaving Adam and Eve in this sad state forever, he prophesies the death of their sin, yes, and their shame too. He gives them a consequence for violating a boundary, yes, *but he also gives them a promise that the consequence isn't forever.*

A Covering

Have you ever had that dream where you're going about your daily business—at school, at work, in the grocery store, on a stage—and you look down and see that you are completely naked?

It's not a unique dream. I would venture to say that most of us have had it. There is something symbolic in the nakedness—the complete and utter exposure to people who have no business seeing us in the dry goods aisle at the local Wal-Mart strutting our stuff.

Contrast this with the way that Adam and Eve started out—naked and unashamed, remember?

But as we saw, eating from the tree of the knowledge of good and evil brought an end to that innocent nakedness. Adam and Eve now had something to hide: their guilt. And so, like all of us try to do at some point, they tried to cover their guilt with something. They wanted a covering to make the exposed sensation—the *bad feeling*—go away.

Remember the fig leaves? I can't imagine they offered much cover from one another, let alone from God's searing vision. But

God is kind yet again: he did not leave them in their fig leaves, throwing his hands up, shrugging his shoulders, and saying, "Serves you right!"

He clothed them.

> The LORD God made clothing from skins for the man and his wife, and he clothed them. (Gen. 3:21)

Even as he drove them out of the garden, he covered their nakedness. He did not make the clothing out of thin air, with the mere sound of his voice, though he certainly could have. He covered them with clothing made "from skins," meaning, animal skins. Given this detail, it's no wonder many commentators believe that God made the very first sacrifice for sin right there in the garden, killing one of the perfect animals he had created to fashion coverings for the shame of his children. After all, the Scriptures tell us, "the wages of sin is death" (Rom. 6:23)—even if the sin happens in a paradise like the garden of Eden.

Do you see how God's fatherly kindness and provision extends to these rebels, even in their worst moment? God could have left them without a promise of future restoration. But he didn't. Right after they rebel against him, he promises them all of this sin and shame is going to be fixed one day. What they did wrong, *he* would make right. And then, on top of that, when he could have just given them this promise—which was gracious enough!—and sent them on their way in their scratchy fig leaves, he instead gives them a temporary covering as they wait for the world to get fixed once and for all.

See, they already know that Someone is coming to repair what sin had marred. God had already promised that by the time we get to the animal skins. But our God is forever using symbols to teach his children. The sacrificing of that first animal which clothed Adam and Eve wasn't merely a nice or utilitarian gesture (though it was certainly kind)—it was showing them a picture of *how* the promise would work itself out. It was showing them that the eventual sacrifice of the promised offspring of the woman—the "Coming One" (Heb. 10:37) who would crush the head of the serpent—would somehow not just handle the guilt and the sin, but cover us and clothe us in righteousness.

Even in these first pages of the Bible, through the slaughtering of an animal to cover Adam and Eve, we see God hinting at something important—something that might free us from all our failure and fear and exposure. And the hint hidden in the Eden story is this: there's something about sacrifice that does away with our shame.

And They All Lived Happily Ever After

And they all lived happily ever after, right?

We all know the answer to that question is a resounding *no*, else several millennia later, I would not be sitting down to write the words in this book. Guilt still abounds in this world. I can't even process the last twenty-four hours of my life without pointing to moments of guilt. And I bet the same goes for you. You and me, we still do wrong things. We still cross the line. Which means that we likely still feel this low-grade level of shame no matter where go, and no matter how many good deeds we try to do to balance out the bad feelings. And because of that shame, we are still hiding.

Which, in turn, means we are still using fig leaves to cover our shame.

Fig leaves are going to be a common theme for us. The beautiful, fan-like foliage was Adam and Eve's garb of choice once they had sinned. Never mind that God can see straight through our flesh and into our hearts—Adam and Eve at least had their swimsuit areas covered, right?

We still find ourselves sewing fig leaves to cover the nakedness and shame that Adam and Eve brought into the world. Whether or not our moments of shame are brought on by personal sin and guilt (or sometimes by things that actually aren't sin at all—but more on that later), we know that Adam and Eve's original sin left its marks on our nature—and left shame in its wake.

Fig leaves are gorgeous, but they make a flimsy outfit choice. Imagine being clothed in a fig leaf during a dust storm—a snowstorm. Imagine being clothed in a fig leaf during a breezy day. Imagine being clothed in a fig leaf when it begins to brown from being disconnected from the plant that made it.

Before we go on, let me ask you: What are your fig leaves? What do you use to cover up the shame you feel on a daily basis? What makes you feel less exposed in front of God and others? When you cross the line, make a mistake, or blow it big time, what do you reach for to make you feel better about your state of guilt? For example, when you pick the kids up late from school, do you do a bunch of dishes when you get back home to feel like you've balanced the score? Then you're probably a person who runs to good works to cover up shame. When you explode on your husband in an argument, do you drown out the mental accusations in your head with episode after episode of your favorite show? (After all, if the characters on TV yell loud enough at each other, perhaps they'll be louder than the voice in your head that's yelling at you.) Then you're probably a person who reaches for indulgence or escapism to deal with shame.

We all have a way we cover our shame. In hopes you'll be brave, I'll whisper the question again: *How do you cover up yours?* Chances are, whatever it is you try to wrap around you in moments of exposure or embarrassment, it's a flimsy covering. It probably feels okay for a second—just long enough to take the edge off the bad feelings. But it doesn't last.

Friend, that's a fig leaf. And it's a shoddy substitute for clothing before a holy God.

And the same way that fig leaves are a shoddy substitute for clothing, shame is a shoddy substitute for repentance.

What does she mean?, you might wonder. Great question.

Repentance or Shame?

Consider when Adam and Eve stood naked before God. When they were not just physically, but spiritually and emotionally bare—he asked them, "Who told you that you were naked?"

I would answer that *shame* told them, because shame is the impulse that made them hide their nakedness. As we've seen before, that's what shame does—it drives us into hiding.

If Adam and Eve had stayed hidden, they would have never heard God's solution to the problem of their own creation. If Adam and Eve had stayed clothed in fig leaves, they would have never understood that they could someday be clothed in a better covering—a covering God himself would provide for them.

But they didn't stay hidden. And they didn't stay clothed in fig leaves.

Instead of remaining hidden or running even further *away* from him in their sin, God beckoned them to move *toward* him. That's what repentance is: coming out into the open *toward* God, letting him speak to your failure, deal with what went wrong, and exchange your flimsy fig leaf for a better covering. Repentance and shame might both have "negative feels" associated with them, but they are different. *Shame moves away from God, which keeps you hidden in sin and left to a flimsy covering—your covering. Repentance moves toward God, who sets you free from sin and gives you a better covering—his covering.*

Shame on You

Here's a natural follow question you may be grappling with: *What exactly is the better covering? How does that shake out, exactly? For Adam and Eve in Genesis it was an animal skin, but how does it work for me, the Christian who feels shame for her sin all the way on the other side of the New Testament?*

Glad you asked. The answer is just around the corner in a parallel chapter (chapter 4, to be specific), so stick with me.

Or, maybe you have an altogether different question. Maybe you're wondering something more along the lines of this:

But what about . . . when I haven't sinned?

What about when shame comes, not as a by-product of wrong-doing, but as a result of living in a fallen world and inhabiting a fallen body? What if we are ashamed because we are still single and all of our friends are married? What if we are ashamed because we are infertile and everyone else seems to have an easy time having children?

What if we are ashamed because we struggle with depression and anxiety and sometimes need some sort of help to climb out of the pit?

What if we're ashamed of putting our kids in public school? What if we're ashamed of being stay-at-home moms? What if we're ashamed of having a job . . . or not having one? What if we're ashamed of our messy living rooms, especially when compared to the perfect living rooms of social media influencers, or compared to our own impossible standards? What if we're ashamed of the limitations that we have because of health or finances?

What if we are ashamed, not because we have failed God's standards as revealed in his Word (i.e., *biblical* standards), but, rather, the standards of others that exist *outside* the Bible (i.e., *extrabiblical* standards)?

This is the balancing act then, friend. Recognizing when shame stems from sin that needs to be repented of . . . and when shame stems from extrabiblical influences that need to be renounced.

Here's the beauty, though: in both instances, the answer to shame is to throw ourselves on the mercy of the God who sees past our nakedness.

Whether we are in sin and need to repent of the guilt that feeds our shame—or we are drowning in expectations that God has never had for us—he *covers our shame*. Every single time.

But how, perhaps you're still wondering. *I'm so tired of living in the shame piling on top of me. So how can I enjoy this covering from God—both when I've sinned and when I haven't? How does it work?*

If it's not an animal skin, what is the "better covering" God offers me when I feel ashamed?

Good thing we're only in chapter 1. Because you're standing on the precipice of an important epiphany. One where you realize a better covering is only *one* part of what you need to effectively deal with shame. What you need from God along with a better covering is a better *image*—and a better *message*, too. And when you realize just how powerful all three of these are when they work together in the gospel for your good, you'll never be the same. Like a person trapped in a mangled car that has crashed, heavy edges bearing down on you and refusing to let up, these three gospel truths taken together have the power to cut through the weight, like the Jaws of Life, and lift shame off of you.

So don't stop now. Yes, you've learned why a better covering is needed. Which means you're already one-third through understanding the problem. Now it's time to learn why you need a better image—because the images you've probably forced yourself to be conformed into? So often, their native language is shame, and the power that keeps you locked into them is fueled by shame too. Which means *they've got to go.*

CHAPTER 2

An Impossible Image That You Can't Attain Anyway

I read *Gone Girl* in 2014, right before my wedding.

My family and fiancé were in Zambia for a month, and I was staying at a friend's house. Normally, my life was crowded with the joyful chaos of eight younger siblings running around, but here, I had a quiet bedroom on the empty upper-floor of some empty-nesters whom I adored.

I stayed up way too late every night reading Gillian Flynn.

I have yet to revisit *Gone Girl*, and I'm sure I've forgotten some parts of the story. But there is one piece of the novel that I remember quite often.

The part about the Cool Girl.

> Men always say that as *the* defining compliment, don't they? *She's a cool girl.* Being the Cool Girl

means that I am a hot, brilliant, funny woman
who adores football, poker, dirty jokes, and burp-
ing, who plays video games . . . [eats] hot dogs and
hamburgers . . . while somehow maintaining a size
2, because Cool Girls are above all, hot. Hot and
understanding. Cool girls never get angry; they
only smile in a chagrined, loving manner, and let
their men do whatever they want. . . . *I don't mind,
I'm the Cool Girl!*[4]

As a young, wide-eyed conservative Christian girl, I could easily recognize the "*unChristian*" parts of the paragraph (a few of
which I've left out here). And so I naturally "bleeped" those out as
I read. But the idea of being *the Cool Girl*—the one who is simulta-
neously everything a man wants her to be and nothing he does not
want her to be—struck me even then. I had never called her by that
name before, but I knew her well. In my own Christian ways, she
was someone I had tried to be for a long time.

I wasn't alone. I've seen that passage referred to many a time by
women from all kinds of different walks of life who related to the
perfect image that Flynn was describing. We all have our version of
"the Cool Girl."

At the time, I didn't even realize how much she was ruling my
own life.

I suppose you could say, in biblical terms, she was a perfect
image I had spent my life trying to be conformed into.

The Time I Tried to Be the Cool Girl

By the time I was twenty, I had a very certain idea of what my life would be.

I would be married by my mid-twenties to the very first man I ever dated. I would homeschool my children and be a stay-at-home mom. My house would stay immaculately polished, and I would have dinner waiting on the table when my husband came home from his nine-to-five. I would forfeit both a college education and a career in pursuit of becoming the very best homemaker I could be.

I'd even taken up knitting.

That whole plan was going swimmingly until I finally hit that "mid-twenties" season, and nothing turned out like it was supposed to.

It was 2012. I was twenty-two. I was in a relationship with someone—let's call him The Boy—and I was naively convinced that he would be the only man I would ever date by the time our relationship got past the "talking to my dad" Christian-courtship phase. He was the first guy who ever showed me affection and said he loved me (on accident, but I counted it). So, when our relationship crashed and burned before the six-month mark, not only was I completely devastated . . . I was ashamed. Because I couldn't get back the months of trying to be his perfect girlfriend. And worse than that, because I clearly couldn't hack it as the Cool Girl.

See, before The Boy and I started dating, I had developed a relationship with his mother. I considered her a Titus 2 mentor of sorts and looked to her to help me develop into a strong Christian woman. Ironically, she was the first person who ever pointed out that I had a bit of a shame problem.

The entire time we were dating, The Boy presented me with a list of traits that his parents (his mother, in particular), deeply desired for me. Every time I failed, he would let me know that his mom was watching, and I really needed to fine-tune my behavior. Every time I spent time around his family, he whispered criticisms and little behavioral modifications that would make them like me more.

The straw that broke the camel's back was, ironically, when his parents cornered us and asked why on earth I was so stiff and nervous around them. Not wanting to betray The Boy's trust, I hemmed and hawed and said something about just being a nervous perfectionist.

The very next day, The Boy called and told me that his mother just didn't think I'd make a very good wife. "She said you told her you're a perfectionist," he said. "That's really not a good quality in a pastor's wife."

(No, dear reader, ten years later, he is not a pastor, nor am I a pastor's wife.)

I was devastated, yes. But more than devastation, as I said before, I felt *shame*. I was the only girl in my friend group who dated more than one boy before getting married. I was the only one who had been dumped. And I was the only one who had to shoulder the awkwardness of a breakup at church every single Sunday, because did I mention The Boy was (like me) one of the other pastor's kids?

I will never forget subsequently sitting down and penning an email to The Boy's mother. Nor will I ever forget her response— which she overlaid with my email in red ink, as though she was having an argument with me in writing. To my very sophomoric, heartfelt email, this woman twice my age replied that my insecurity had been my own undoing.

I can't erase this one line from my memory—the one that said, "It would appear that you were crushed under the weight of your own doubt and fears. Don't blame me for that."

At the time, her words felt like such a slap in the face—especially since I'd been vulnerable with her about the weight of the shame and personal expectations that I so often felt. But, a decade later, I have realized that the words that seemed meant to wound me . . . were true.

No, I did not ask, at twenty-two, to be a marionette yanked around by a somewhat spiritually abusive elder's wife. But I also didn't have enough of a sense of myself to stop letting The Boy use his mother's expectations to manipulate me (even if that was not his intent). I didn't have enough sense to realize shame was probably pulling him around on a leash too.

I didn't have enough sense to stop hammering myself into the image of the Cool Girl.

The Christian Cool Girl

I wonder what your upbringing taught you about the Cool Girl. What does her image look like, to you? Maybe you were taught she's a boss in a boardroom who climbed her way to the top, always dominates the meeting, and leaves the other employees in amazement every time she weighs in on an idea. Or perhaps the influences in your life painted her as a free-spirited artist in a big city, whose creativity knows no bounds, whose schedule bows to no one, and whose outfit always looks effortlessly fashionable. Or maybe you were simply taught that she's woman a step ahead of you in life. You know, the one with the husband you still don't have. Or the kid you still don't have. Or the house you still don't have. Or the perfect job—the one that lets her use all her gifts—that you, again, still don't have.

See, we've all been taught to become some version of the Cool Girl. But that's not all. At some point you and I became a Christian, right? Which means we added Christian values to the Cool Girl in some way, and now she's an elusive, hodgepodge Super Woman of sorts who always seems to have a nagging presence in the back of our mind.

For me, the Cool Girl of my upbringing was different from Flynn's worldly version, but she was cool all the same. Like Flynn's Cool Girl, she was hot—but she knew that modest was hottest. She was a virgin, totally innocent to the sexual ways of the world— but somehow, in the span of mere hours on her wedding day, she would be magically prepared to make all her husband's wildest (and even pornographic) fantasies come true upon their wedding night and every night after that. She was brilliant enough to homeschool prodigies, but not brilliant enough for her husband to learn anything from her. She knew that her place was in the home, and made jokes about joyfully submitting to her man that would make the worldly girls *cringe*. She could cook, clean, and sew. She could run a tight ship—but never came off as "wound up" about it. She could do all the stuff in Proverbs 31 except, of course, "considering a field and buying it" or "selling her goods at the city gate" because those things would require business savvy and business-stuff was only for the boys. So scratch those verses.

The Cool Girl also had time to groom the dog, make meals for neighbors, host the ministry people, read all the most important books, spend hours in the Bible every morning, spend an equal amount of time teaching the kids every day, polish the silverware, keep up with PTA and homework, get her hair and nails done regularly, clip the coupons, get the oil changed, handle the bills, plan the family outings, maintain a garden, lead the book club, work out every day to keep that perfect figure, handle the bedtime routine with the little ones and cover all the weekend hours with them too (because Dad was too tired to be present), serve in the church, and while she was at it, disciple ten or more women at a very deep level on a weekly basis. *All without needing any help.* (Also all while likely being pregnant or breastfeeding a child in between each task.)

And she was also understanding. Her past had to be a clean slate, but if her husband's past was a bit marred, that was okay because "boys will be boys" and "girls will be understanding." On top of this, she never broke down in front of her husband or asked him to take on any of these tasks. It was her job to soothe away the family's woes, handle the stress so he didn't have to see it, and make things work so he didn't have to get involved with his own children's needs (or hers, for that matter). Oh, and she never got angry; she only smiled in a chagrined, loving manner and while teaching her kids self-control over their instincts, let her man follow his every instinct and do whatever he wanted . . . *I don't mind! I'm a virtuous woman!*

Depending on your Christian subculture, you may not recognize my (exhausting!) image of the Cool Girl, but that's the thing—this fantasy can be molded to fit whatever your subculture's desire commands. Because the Cool Girl is, above all, an invention—not a reality. As we alluded to before, she's a Frankenstein's monster of sorts, made up of some good things that are genuinely biblical and some other convoluted (or even sinful) things that stem from her surrounding culture. And mixing the two never goes well, as we'll see in a moment.

The Power of Shame

Whether she's bringing home the bacon and frying it in the pan or frying it in the pan while she's barefoot and pregnant, we know what it is to have the image of the ideal Christian woman looming in our minds. So what is it, exactly, that forces us to meet that ideal? What keeps us conformed into her image, even when it's obviously not a good image, even when it's an image comprised of both godly and ungodly elements, and even when we obviously don't—and *can't*—squeeze into it?

Shame does. Shame has that kind of power. It can keep you living in a whole identity that isn't even real. Squirm as you may to try to break free from the silhouette of this icon no woman can actually be, the fear of shame shoves you right back into it. It lurks in the shadows, threatening to punish you if you step outside of the mold or don't measure up to the standards. The fear of being shamed whispers: "If you step outside of this identity, even just a little, and let it be seen that you can't fit the bill or you can't pull it all off, you'll lose everything. *You'll be cast out.* You'll lose your reputation. Your place in your circle of friends. Your status as a good mom. Your reputation as a desirable wife. Your value as a Christian and even a human being. Better to identify as the Cool Girl and force yourself to be conformed into her image than confess to the world—or to God—who you really are and then lose it all." And just like that, shame has given you a name and threatens you at every turn to live up to it.

There are many weapons to choose from if the goal is to get people to conform to something, and shame is one of the most powerful. And you know what? We use it on ourselves every day.

Why?

Made in His Image

To answer that question, let's consider Eve's story again, and then let's move forward from Eve to the people who eventually descended from her: Israel.

Think back to the dawn of creation. Adam and Eve inhabited the garden, completely free of shame. They had everything they could ever need: food, shelter, purpose, and companionship—not just with one another, but with the God of the universe. All kinds of trees and foliage presented themselves as good to eat, and Adam and Eve had never known hunger—only satisfaction.

But a serpent was on the prowl.

> Now the serpent was the most cunning of all the wild animals that the LORD God had made. He said to the woman, "Did God really say, 'You can't eat from any tree in the garden'?" (Gen. 3:1)

Cleverly, the serpent ups the stakes. He knows good and well that God did not forbid *every* tree in the garden. But he also knows the power of perverting God's commands into exacting legalism. God's commands are not burdensome to those who love him (1 John 5:3); his yoke is easy; his burden is light (Matt. 11:28–30). But Satan is wily. He *knows* that his pathway leads to death while God's path leads to life; but he also knows how easy it is to mix truth with just a little bit of a lie—all so we might be persuaded into thinking God's commands are burdensome.

So instead of asking Eve the question he wanted to ask her (perhaps, "What would it take to get you to eat from that tree?"), he asks her why her God's commands are so unreasonable. Eve's response is also telling:

> The woman said to the serpent, "We may eat the fruit from the trees in the garden. But about the fruit of the tree in the middle of the garden, God said, 'You must not eat it or touch it, or you will die.'" (Gen. 3:2–3)

Whether intentionally or not, she has also upped the stakes. God *did* say that if Adam and Eve *ate* from the fruit of the tree in the middle of the garden, they would surely die (Gen. 2:17). However, he didn't say anything about *touching* the tree.

Do you see how easy it is to make God's law seem like a burden? Do you see how simple it is to supplant his holy law with the petulant demands of an unreasonable taskmaster? Do you see the pathway that shame can take into our hearts by making his commands seem *impossible* for us to keep?

We've already seen how the story ends:

> "No! You will certainly not die," the serpent said to the woman. "In fact, God knows that when you eat it your eyes will be opened and you will be like God, knowing good and evil." The woman saw that the tree was good for food and delightful to look at, and that it was desirable for obtaining wisdom. So she took some of its fruit and ate it;

she also gave some to her husband, who was with
her, and he ate it. Then the eyes of both of them
were opened, and they knew they were naked; so
they sewed fig leaves together and made coverings
for themselves. (Gen. 3:4–7)

"See how burdensome God's commands are?" Satan whispered.
"See how he's holding out on you? See how he doesn't want to give
you all good things?"

We could paint Eve as a swashbuckling heroine who just wants
to know more—but that would be neglecting the fact that she had
access to the very knowledge of the God of the universe. She knew
God. We could paint Eve as wanting to aspire to a higher calling
than the one God had given her—but she was made *in his very
image.* She (and Adam) was made to (like God) benevolently rule
and reign over the entire earth. There is no greater calling. There
is no better version of herself that could possibly exist. There's no
greater image to be conformed into. And yet now here she is, thinking there could be.

The sin of Eve wasn't wanting too much; it was wanting too
little. She not only had access to the God who created everything in
existence, her very internal makeup was made in his likeness. And
yet, instead, she looked out on the horizon with the idea that some
other image of herself was out there, in need of discovering—a version she thought was evolved and "more" of herself than the current
version. But that future version of herself out there who knew not
just good, but evil too? It was actually *de*volved.

An example here would be the way you feel about a beloved
person in your life who struggles with addiction. As they know
more of the evil that comes with addictive substances, they wither

away, body and soul. They lose themselves, and when you talk to them, you wish you could take them by the shoulders and say, "My dear friend, every time you know more of this evil, you're becoming less of yourself. How can you not see?"

In choosing to believe the serpent about the knowledge of good and evil, Eve chose to be less of herself, less than the fullness God had for her, and when she did, do you know what was waiting for her?

Shame.

She thought this decision would lead her to being even more like God—to greater honor. And yet, to chase some other image actually led her to being cast out from his presence—to shame. To an experience she was never built to bear.

How about you? Have you ever tried to take matters into your own hands instead of trusting that you serve a God who has your best interest at heart? Have you supplanted his will for your life by adding extra requirements to his Word and thereby creating a legalistic caricature that is impossible to attain? Have you ever taken the path that you thought required less trust in God, only to be set adrift without him? Have you ever thought there was some better calling, or some better image to be conformed into than his?

I have.

And Eve certainly did.

And we know the consequences of her sin.

Making Our Own Images

Hundreds of years later, Adam and Eve's offspring would become a mighty nation. Remember God's promise in Genesis 3:15? Someone was coming to do away with shame *forever*. And that Someone would be born from the seed of the woman, through a nation fathered by Abraham. That nation would be preserved through both individuals and corporately until the answer to our shame and suffering would be born.

Along the way, they were enslaved by the Egyptians for four hundred years. In several miraculous displays of his might, God led the Israelites out of slavery. By the time they had gotten to the desert between Egypt and the Promised Land, they had witnessed ten plagues, plundered gold from the Egyptians, and walked across dry land while the Red Sea stood at attention at either side of them.

You would think God had earned their trust.

But then, Eve had seen God with her own eyes and *still* took the word of a talking snake over him, so we shouldn't be surprised at where this story is going.

Moses went up to Mount Sinai to receive the law of God, and Israel got restless. Their security in God began to wane, and they started looking for some kind of substitute. And here we see where another story about *image* comes to us, front and center, with many lessons to learn.

> When the people saw that Moses delayed in coming down from the mountain, they gathered around Aaron and said to him, "Come, make gods for us who will go before us because this Moses, the man who brought us up from the land of Egypt—we don't know what has happened to him!" (Exod. 32:1)

Their words to Aaron are not exactly accurate. True, Moses has been on Mount Sinai for about eight chapters at this point.

But he left instructions for them before he went (Exod. 24:14), and a cloud hovered over the mountain to signify Moses's ongoing conversation to God (vv. 16–17). So, although forty days and forty nights probably felt like a long time, and though the cloud probably seemed far away from their vantage point, *they actually do know what's happened to him.* Not to mention they have been well taken care of in Moses's absence—they are fed through manna from heaven, after all (Exod. 16).

Instead of reminding Israel of these truths, however, Aaron acquiesces to their commands:

> Aaron replied to them, "Take off the gold rings that are on the ears of your wives, your sons, and your daughters and bring them to me." So all the people took off the gold rings that were on their ears and brought them to Aaron. He took the gold from them, fashioned it with an engraving tool, and **made it into an image** of a calf.
>
> Then they said, "Israel, these are your gods, who brought you up from the land of Egypt!"
>
> When Aaron saw this, he built an altar in front of it and made an announcement: "There will be a festival to the LORD tomorrow." Early the next morning they arose, offered burnt offerings, and presented fellowship offerings. The people sat down to eat and drink, and got up to party. (Exod. 32:2–6)

The cow was a powerful idol in Egypt, and Israel had returned to what she knew (not for the first time since leaving slavery). She doubted God's goodness, she doubted the vessel that was Moses, and she descended into idol worship that eventually led to shame and separation from the Father.

Do you see a pattern here? Do you see how, when we doubt the provision and precepts of the Lord, we take matters into our own hands and leave ourselves wide open for shame's corrupting influence when our sin is ultimately exposed?

And on top of that, do you see the mixture of godly and ungodly practices in this story—the pattern of adding something else to what God has instructed? We see certain aspects of their idol worship that are based in God's Word—festivals, burnt offerings, and fellowship offerings, for example. These were required of them in God's law. In our day and time, we'd call these *biblical*. But making a graven image of a calf and then worshipping it as the deliverer who brought them out of Egypt? *That* didn't come from God's Word—it came from their surrounding culture.

And yet here they are, mixing the two and calling it godly. Just as it went in Eden, they believe they can keep some of the truth while adding in some lies.

So it goes when we worship the wrong image—whether that's the Cool Girl, or marriage, children, a successful career, or a pristine reputation. Whatever it is for you, I know three things. One, it's probably something you've forged with your own resources. Just as an idol in Israel's day demanded their gold, yours probably demands a precious resource that you willingly and frequently hand over to it. Two, it is probably something you've crafted when you got bored with waiting on God for something. And three, it's probably some image made up of both biblical and unbiblical elements, and yet you worship it all the same, calling it godly.

I don't have to tell you what this image is for me; you already know. It's the Cool Girl. What is it for you? And how long have you pursued it before you were overcome with shame?

Let's look at one more example.

The Cool Nations

Israel has made it out of the wilderness now. They are establishing themselves as a nation. That law God gave Moses on Mount Sinai while they were impatiently causing calves to jump out of the fire (see Exodus 32:24, and note that just as in Adam and Eve's story, blame-shifting accompanies shame) has governed the nation for another few hundred years.

At this point, they are a theocracy: a people overseen by God as their ruler. And they have a way to hear from God directly: the prophets. Yet they aren't content with this setup. Like Eve, they look out on the horizon and see some other image of themselves that they're *sure* will be better and more evolved. Like their ancestors who made the golden calf, they take their cues on what this version of themselves should look like not by looking *up* to God but looking *around* at surrounding culture, adding some of the elements they see *over there* to their current, God-given situation *right here*. To be specific, they look around and decide that they want to emulate the other nations in a particular way: they want a king.

> So all the elders of Israel gathered together and went to Samuel at Ramah. They said to him, "Look, you are old, and your sons do not walk in your ways. Therefore, appoint a king to judge us

the same as all the other nations have." (1 Sam. 8:4–5)

They thought the other nations were a better version of what God had directed them to be. They wanted God, and they wanted their people to walk in God's ways, but they wanted to be like the Cool Nations too, assuming the cultural norm of an earthly king would do a better job at that than God would. They were paying more attention to cultural norms around them than they were to God's Word, and they were letting their surroundings tell them what it meant to be "a nation" instead of obeying God's definitions and instructions.

Again, we have people flouting the wise provision of God (every good tree in the garden; the law of Moses; his plans for leadership) to reflect an image that God *never* asked them to reflect. And God even reminded them of this. He gave them a clear warning that this strategy of fitting themselves into the mold of other nations wouldn't go well. He tells them that the king on the horizon would only take from them, would only make them less of themselves, would only cause them to cry out to God for relief. But they wouldn't listen. They wanted to be ruled "like all the other nations" (1 Sam. 8:10–20).

They traded the glory of God's calling on their nation for the fancy infrastructure they saw around them—because they were ashamed of what God had called that ragtag smattering of little tribes to be.

Have you been ashamed of God's actual calling on your life as grounded in his Word because it didn't match up with the right kind of cultural label? Have you been tempted to trade his wise and personal leadership in your life for a yoke of shame and comparison? Have you ever looked out onto the horizon, assuming if you add a dash of societal values and expectations to your image, you'll be "more" of yourself—that you'll finally reach some perfect silhouette—only to find yourself crying out to God for relief?

Me too.

A Good Woman

Do you see what's happening here? In each case, neither Eve nor Israel relies on what God actually told them about themselves. In each case, there's some mold they assume they're supposed to fill that was never meant for them to squeeze into. For Eve, there was an original mold custom-made for her that knew no evil and felt no burden. For Israel, there was a sacred space for them to fill in this world and it wasn't fashioned after the way the surrounding nations looked. And yet both of them chose some other "ideal" that subsequently locked them not only into some image that wasn't fitting, but into shame.

And we can make that same mistake when it comes to our ideals about what it means to be a *good* woman. While we have the abundance that God has laid forth for us in his Word at our fingertips (not just in Titus 2, 1 Peter 3:1–6, or Proverbs 31, but in the *entire counsel of Scripture*), we choose instead to listen to Satan's voice who whispers "*Did God really say?*" in our ears. We choose to reach outside of what God has said, and we start looking around, adding to what he's said with whatever this tribe or that tribe says is the standard. Before long, we not only begin to worship this piecemeal goddess as an icon, we also do what everyone does when they worship an idol—we start hammering ourselves into her likeness day by day, trying desperately to shape ourselves into her mold, the hammer being the weapon of shame.

My piecemeal goddess, as I've said *ad nauseum* at this point, is the Christian Cool Girl. She promises there's more on the horizon and demands all my resources only to turn around and make me less of myself. And hammering myself into her image exhausts me to such a degree that I'm ready to throw my hands up in frustration and blame God for calling me to standards that he *never* wrote down in his Word. And the further away from his Word I get, tempted away from it by the enemy, the more I shame-spiral over that woman that God never truly called me to be.

Here's the bottom line: whether we are Eve trying to be some better version of herself, or Israel trying to fit the mold of other nations, or women in today's age trying to force ourselves into the image of the Cool Girl, there is a reason we allow shame to shove us into a mold that doesn't fit—*we truly believe it's a better, truer, more attainable image than the image God has built us to be conformed into.*

The Answer

Aren't you ready for that—to find a better image, a better vision, of who you are supposed to be? I know I am. Because here's the thing: I'm tired of the Christian Cool Girl. Like, I want to find her and tie her down to the nearest railroad tracks.

It's not as violent an idea as it sounds, because, let's remember . . . she doesn't exist.

Some of us spend our entire adult lives masquerading as her or attempting to become her, or judging women who are *not* her because that's the best way to hide that we aren't her either.

She paralyzes me. And I bet she does the same to you.

When I think about the shame stories women tend to share with one another—often akin to my story with The Boy—the answers they give each other are usually on either side of a spectrum. Some say if you just hammer harder, you'll finally make it. You'll finally be squished into the image of the Cool Girl (whoever that is for their group of friends), and you'll be happy. The answer here is just to double down, grit your teeth, and if you put in enough work, you can be formed into whatever image you want to be. *The image of the Cool Girl is awesome—just put in more effort.*

The answer on the other end of the spectrum is to look within for the power it will take to unlearn your instinct to fit into *any* mold. The goal here is to throw off all expectations and get rid of the idea of an "image" altogether. *There's no "image" you should be conforming yourself into or "right way" you should be in this world— you need to kill that instinct STAT and just do whatever feels right to you in the moment.*

As I've grown, I see now that the answer for the debacle with The Boy was neither of these extremes. The answer was not to try even harder to become the Cool Girl. After all, she's not real. Nor was the answer to totally kill my instinct to be conformed into a good image. After all, every human being feels the unquenchable desire to move toward a vision of who they are supposed to be. The whole reason we feel the insatiable desire toward an ideal image is because the image of God itself was marred at the fall—not destroyed, but distorted. And we can sense this deep down. We know we're not what we should be, and we long to be recreated into something glorious. To *become* something better. To change, to grow, to move toward a whole and perfect state of some kind.

Nothing and no one can shut down such a deep instinct in the human heart.

So the answer for me, I realized, wasn't to conform into the image of the Cool Girl with some extra effort. Nor was it to kill the whole category of "image."

The answer was to kill the Cool Girl and find a better image to be conformed into.

What the Cool Girl Misses

The Boy and I are both married now. Not to each other. We both have families of our own. And I'm not angry with him. I know firsthand that, by the grace of growth, a boy who wounded one woman can go on to build up another. I do not believe that my experience of The Boy says much about the man he is today.

I am a woman who has largely been shaped by shame where I should have been shaped by the truth of the gospel that I have been hearing my entire life. I am a woman with deep wounds, some of which have been inflicted by the expectations of others . . . but wounds that I did not have the good sense to try to shield myself from, or shy away from.

I am a woman who has been called to *abundance* in spite of that hurt, and who experiences it every day, on the other side of the shame-spirals that used to define me. I am a woman who ditched the Cool Girl and is now being conformed into a better, a *perfect* image—one that's actually possible to move toward, and actually makes me a truer and better person (which, yes, we'll explore in coming chapters).

I want that for you too.

CHAPTER 3

Three False Gospels That Can't Get the Shame Off

E very time I talk about shame, it sets off red flags for at least one person who's listening.

Isn't shame the thing that keeps society from descending into abject chaos? Shame stops us from walking around naked—from public lewdness—from all manner of criminal activity. It's that thing that reins in the depravity of mankind by making him aware of the fact that if he steps too far out of line, he will be ostracized. Shameless people are sociopaths, right? The ones who feel no compunction when they commit whatever eerie crime you're binging on your latest *True Crime* podcast. Put another way, you could say that sometimes the fear of being shamed restrains evil in this world—it reins in the crazy.

And you know what? I'd agree with you.

It's true that the fear of shame offers a rudimentary sort of check and balance to society. I believe this is a by-product of a conscience that was made in God's image, even if that conscience doesn't acknowledge God.

Consider this passage in Romans:

> For God's wrath is revealed from heaven against all godlessness and unrighteousness of people who by their unrighteousness suppress the truth, since what can be known about God is evident among them, because God has shown it to them. For his invisible attributes, that is, his eternal power and divine nature, have been clearly seen since the creation of the world, being understood through what he has made. As a result, people are without excuse. (Rom. 1:18–20)

As we can see, Romans 1 tells the story of a people who *know* the truth that there is a God but suppress that truth. It tells the story of a people who look around at creation and see the evidence of a Creator in everything that lives and moves. It tells the story of the descendants of Adam and Eve hearkening back to the understanding of their first mother and father: that God made the world, and when he made it, it was good.

This knowledge, Romans 2 tells us, is written on their hearts:

> They show that the work of the law is written on their hearts. Their consciences confirm this. Their competing thoughts either accuse or even excuse them. (v. 15)

What does this mean? It means that we know, deep in our bones, there's a God we'll have to answer to one day, giving an account of our lives. It means that our conscience is well aware of him, and our failure to live up to his standards and his glory, and our inability to last very long in his pure presence, but our minds tend to handle the witness of our conscience by muzzling it, despairing over it, or explaining it away so that we don't have to experience the shame associated with facing the truth. It means that, should we even be granted the grace to pay mind to what our conscience is trying to tell us, in nestles that deep, heavy and foreboding feeling, like when Miss Clavel of *Madeline* fame sits up in her bed and utters, "Something is not right."

And this is where the shame creeps in. That feeling of wanting to hide our faces in the presence of a holy God is a *right* feeling. When faced with the presence of God, the prophet Isaiah quaked and uttered:

> Woe is me for I am ruined
> because I am a man of unclean lips
> and live among a people of unclean lips,
> and because my eyes have seen the King,
> the LORD of Armies. (Isa. 6:5)

Even a man who had devoted his life to the proclamation of the Word of God felt every inch of his unworthiness in the presence of that God. That feeling of complete nakedness that Adam and Eve felt, that hankering for fig leaves, that yearning to hide—that is a natural reaction to being thrust into the presence of a king.

Imagine: you're at home in your pajamas. Maybe there are smatterings of pimple cream on your face. Perhaps you haven't brushed your teeth just yet. You are disheveled and egg-and-coffee stained from making breakfast.

The doorbell rings.

You want to run to the back and get a bit more presentable, but the ringing comes again. And again. After a moment, it is so insistent that you throw your hands up in despair, march to the door, and swing it open to reveal . . .

You fill in the blank.

The president of the United States. Your favorite movie star. The band you listened to on a constant loop as a teen. The love of your life—the one that got away. Make the image work however you must—bring someone back from the dead if need be. Is it Cecily Tyson? Is it Gandhi? Is it Elvis?

Whoever it is, your hand flies up to the hair that's piled into a three-day-old messy bun on top of your head. You move to clutch your robe around that ratty pajama top. You gulp, fighting the urge to do a quick smell test on your breath.

Maybe you completely freak out and slam the door, because *Idris Elba cannot see me like this!*

That unworthiness you feel in the face of whoever you filled in the blank with? Multiply that by innumerable *millions* and you have a mere fraction of what Isaiah felt standing in front of God.

Or, perhaps think of a different scenario. Same wardrobe. Same insistent ringing of the doorbell. Same tossing it open to reveal your guest. But this time, it's someone you've wronged and never gotten the chance to apologize to.

It's the girl you snubbed at school. It's the boy you teased so much that he stopped leaving his house. It's the boyfriend or girlfriend whose heart you broke irrevocably, out of your own sense of selfishness or pride. It's . . .

Fill in that blank. Fill in that blank with a person who has every right to loathe you because of how awful you were to them. Fill in that blank with a person whose forgiveness you crave, but feel you can never ask for. Fill in that blank with someone you've wronged.

That warmth in your cheeks? The sinking in your stomach?

My friend, *that* is shame.

Shouldn't We Feel Shame?

Okay, so *shouldn't* you feel ashamed when you've wronged someone?

Yes, it is a completely normal and moral reaction. Paul doesn't hold back on the heaping helping of disgrace (a cousin of shame) that is deserved by those who see God's glory in creation and choose not to glorify him:

> For though they knew God, they did not glorify him as God or show gratitude. Instead, their thinking became worthless, and their senseless hearts were darkened. Claiming to be wise, they became fools and exchanged the glory of the immortal God for images resembling mortal man, birds, four-footed animals, and reptiles. Therefore God delivered them over in the desires of their hearts to sexual impurity, so that their bodies were degraded among themselves. They exchanged the truth of God for a lie, and worshiped and served what has been created instead of the Creator, who

is praised forever. Amen. For this reason God
delivered them over to disgraceful passions. (Rom.
1:21–26a)

Fools ought to be ashamed of themselves. We recognize that.
And so when a writer like me says, "We need to rid ourselves of this
crippling shame," what you might mistakenly hear is, "We need to
walk around *glad* that we're a bunch of idolatrous fools."

But look at Isaiah.

There he is, quaking in the throne room of the God of the
universe. Not only is he unworthy by sheer nature of the fact that
God exists in perfectly holy perfection—he's also unworthy because
he is a sinner. Because of the sin of his forefather, Adam, Isaiah has
inherited a nature that is wholly *other* than God's. It is bound by
unrighteousness, and even the good works Isaiah does are like filthy
rags before God's righteousness (Isa. 64:6).

Have you ever felt this way before? Have you ever felt completely unworthy? Not just underdressed, but utterly exposed?

I certainly have. In fact, the memory flashing before my mind
right now boasts a lot more levity than Isaiah's predicament, but
I felt so much shame in that moment that if I close my eyes and
think on it, I can feel the blush creeping back up my cheeks.

I am a classically trained pianist.

Or, I *was* until my freshman year in college, when three-hour-
a-day practices caused a carpal tunnel flare that put me out of commission for six months. When I came back to the piano, it just
never felt the same, and more than a decade later, my repertoire
consists of snippets of Debussy, memories of Bach, and maybe
some *Chopsticks* or *Heart and Soul* if I'm lucky.

But back in high school, I was a pianist to such a degree that I played a couple of concerts. These concerts weren't solo affairs. They took place on stage with about twenty other pianists, all playing the exact same duet at the same time. For my nerdy homeschool self, and my awkward nonathletic self, it was my little yearly Super Bowl.

For these performances, all of us girls wore the exact same dress. It was always some polyester something that could've come from Grandma's closet, and this year was no different. The day of our first performance, I pulled it on and complained about the large, ornate buttons that marched down the front of the dress.

At least everyone was wearing the same thing.

My family arrived to the venue early, so I shuffled to my seat at the very beginning of the row, sat down, and waited.

And as I waited, I began to feel uncomfortable. Because as the rest of the girls walked into the venue, I saw that their dresses were the same plum pudding color as mine was, but an entirely different cut. My mind flashed back to the catalogue we all ordered our dresses from, and my heart sank as I surmised that I must have picked the wrong dress. So now, not only was I the only Black girl in our ensemble—I was the only one in this hideous dress with the buttons.

By the time the entire row had filled, I was taking deep, cleansing breaths to calm my nerves, both about the performance and about flubbing my dress order. That's when I felt my mom's familiar touch on my shoulder. I turned to see her face contorted in a mask of horror.

"We need to go to the bathroom," she whispered.

That's when I glanced at the girl next to me, who was trying not to stare. I realized it at the same moment that I stood on shaky legs and my mom said it:

"Your dress is on backwards."

The walk from my seat on the far corner of the front row *all the way to the exit* felt like it took an eternity. But it was nothing compared to the walk back. As a teenager, for all intents and purposes, my life was over. Not only had I had my dress on backwards—but I was also clearly aware of my mistake and had tried to casually fix it in the ladies' room. I wanted to cry. I wanted to die. I wanted to run.

My mom's firm hand on my shoulder told me that I didn't really have any of those options. She steered me as far as the first row, and then gave me a squeeze and headed back to her seat. I walked to that far corner chair like Joan of Arc on the way to be burned at the stake. I sat between a girl who I only knew by sight, because I was painfully shy during our weeks of practice, and my piano teacher's son.

"I totally thought the buttons went in the front," she whispered. "If it's possible to make this dress look good, it looks better that way."

I turned to my piano teacher's son, who didn't have any words of comfort, but flipped his eyelids to make me laugh.

And I eased back into my seat.

Okay, so maybe you know how to decipher the back of a dress from the front of the dress (yes, friend, it had tags and everything), but I'd wager that you also know what it's like to feel, first, the pang of shame, and then its relieving unburdening as the people you were ashamed to face welcome you with open arms. You walk into the situation thinking you'll be met with all of the horror you've imagined, but instead, you're met with warmth.

Isaiah felt this horror on a much deeper level than teenage Jasmine. Which, given the level of my hormonal theatrics, is as deep as it goes. His first word upon being thrust into the presence of God? "Woe."

Not, *woah* as in, "Wow! Awesome! Tubular!"

No, *woe* as in, distress at the sight of impending doom. He wasn't afraid of being laughed out of the throne room—he realized that the risk was far greater than that. Because of his unworthiness, he could be cast out of the very presence of God.

And the response of the angels around him?

> Then one of the seraphim flew to me, having in his hand a burning coal that he had taken with tongs from the altar. And he touched my mouth and said: "Behold, this has touched your lips; your guilt is taken away, and your sin atoned for."
> (Isa. 6:6–7 ESV)

Here we see the angels come toward Isaiah, bearing something that can provide a way for him to stand before God: a burning coal. After the burning coal takes care of the problem (more on that later), the angel leaves him with a message of good news: guilt is gone; sin, atoned for. Here we see that the angels didn't just make Isaiah *feel* better. He *was* better for whatever had occurred between him and his God in that throne room.

Isaiah's shame wasn't just comforted or coddled, like mine was. The message that Isaiah received from the angel is that his shame was *removed*.

Here's the thing about removing shame, though: it's not a unique proposition. Everywhere you turn, there is a lifestyle guru, blogger, social media influencer, or podcaster giving you advice on how to loosen the chains of shame on your life.

I don't know what flavor it is for you—maybe it's the mom-shaming thing or the body-image-shaming thing or the single-girl-shaming thing or even religious forms of shaming. Maybe you're a woman of color who has felt shame for not fitting into a white evangelical mold of femininity. Regardless of which version of it you struggle with, there's always a "prophet" with a "message" around every corner, promising to help you find the truest and best way to remove the bad feelings associated with shame. We could even call these messages "gospels," for they try to proclaim a way out of the existential shame we all feel. And the gospel-bearers are like a bad version of the angel in Isaiah 6, meaning, they come with a message about removing your shame, yes, but the messages they bear aren't really good news. Why? Because their shame-removal methods don't actually work. Examples of these gospels abound, but here are the ones I see spreading the quickest among American evangelical women.

Three Faulty "Gospels"

Message #1: Shake It Off

The first message the world will invite us to believe is this one: *shake off any and all feelings of shame. Be shameless.* The logic goes like this: If you feel bad feelings about something, no matter what it is or why you did it, the problem is that you even feel bad about it in the first place. So stop feeling bad about something that you wanted to do! If you want to do it, do it. Nobody has the right to tell you it's wrong. You shouldn't feel shame for violating boundaries because there's no such thing as a boundary to begin with! Do whatever you want, be free, and don't feel bad about it. You're perfect just the way you are—in all your desires, your motives, your appetites, and your decisions. And girl, if you're perfect, who can judge you? Nobody! Do you!

In this message, rather than staring our shame in the face like Isaiah did ("woe is me"), we're told to cast it aside without examination. This way of looking at things essentially believes that bad feelings do nothing but cramp our style and our sense of identity, and since shame is a bad feeling, we should throw it out wholesale. Instead of the bad feeling *maybe* being conviction over sin, it's actually judgmental haters or the patriarchy trying to shove us down a few rungs on the ladder.

The problem with this message for the Christian is that in the Bible, the whole "conviction over sin" thing is kind of an important ingredient to getting right with God, and the idea that we're perfect the way we are just doesn't tell the truth about reality when we look around the world. If all people are perfect just the way they are, the *world* would be perfect. But it's not. People, including you and me, do terrible things. Held up next to God, we aren't perfect at all. Think of Isaiah. He didn't just stand in the throne room and say, "Hey, God, I know you're the matchless king of the universe, but I'm going to walk in my truth and you're going to be cool with it, okay?"

This message of the world might call us to be unapologetically shameless, but have you thought about what might happen in a truly *shameless* society? It would have zero checks and balances. What would that even look like? Maybe you think of Woodstock, free love, shirts optional, drugs perfuming the air. Or perhaps you think of Gotham, crime capital of the world, with the bat signal as its only hope.

Or if you grew up in Sunday school, maybe you think of Sodom and Gomorrah, or the preflood world that God wiped clean to start fresh with Noah. Maybe your mind floats back, once more, to Romans:

> There is no one righteous, not even one.
> There is no one who understands;
> there is no one who seeks God.
> All have turned away;
> all alike have become worthless.
> There is no one who does what is good,
> not even one.
> Their throat is an open grave;
> they deceive with their tongues.
> Vipers' venom is under their lips.
> Their mouth is full of cursing and bitterness.
> Their feet are swift to shed blood;
> ruin and wretchedness are in their paths,
> and the path of peace they have not known.
> There is no fear of God before their eyes.
> (Rom. 3:10–18)

The people described here *ought* to be ashamed of themselves, right? Especially if they have any sort of moral compass. Deceiving, shedding blood, bitterness, wretchedness, no peace, and no fear of God sounds *exactly* what will happen to a culture who gets rid of shame on a wholesale level.

In fact, the primary prophets of casting off shame seem to be the very same people who are casting off Christianity for its moral implications. If we throw out all the shame in our lives, what is to stop us from throwing out Christianity altogether? Isn't the very law that keeps us in line the thing that *produces* our shame?

But that's just it. We are *born* ashamed because we are *born* fallen and, therefore, unworthy to stand in the presence of a holy God (Ps. 51:5). Because of Adam's sin, we are *all* shaped by sin (Rom. 5:12) and, therefore, *all* born with a proclivity toward hiding our unworthiness behind whatever fig leaves we can cover ourselves up with to make ourselves feel more acceptable and put-together (piano recitals and all). Before we even understand the law, we understand shame in the form of embarrassment. Three-year-old Jasmine combing Mommy's hair did not know the Ten Commandments, but she knew what it felt like to want to hide.

If we isolate shame from the broader narrative of creation, we run the risk of destroying it . . . and our moral compass in the process.

Here's what I mean by that: living shamelessly is only a viable option for humankind *to an extent*. Most of us would agree that when certain shameless urges become actions that harm others, they are no longer viable options for a safe and fruitful society.

Let me give an example.

According to some moral compasses in our day and age, adultery is okay in certain circumstances—like if the adulterer is in an abusive marriage, or has found true love after years in a loveless relationship. But those *same* moral compasses might frown on, say, serial affairs that harm a loving spouse. They might heap shame on this person who is harming their spouse by repeated unfaithfulness.

According to others, though, the shame heaped on a habitual cheater needs to be done away with just like the shame on, say, working moms. It's all shame after all. And it's all stopping us from having the desires that we want, right? In this line of thinking, we're all perfect just the way we are, including whatever desires we find "natural." Love is love, and shame is shame is shame, the reasoning goes—and so we should indiscriminately throw off that shame no matter *why* we feel it or what form it takes. Whether it's heaped on the serial adulterer or the unmarried woman or the low-income worker, it's got to go.

My example purposefully compares one level of severity with a higher level, because I believe when confronted with higher levels, people can better see the folly of doing away with the concept of shame altogether. If a sense of shame over wrongdoing isn't guiding us, won't we be led instead by our desires? And doesn't the end of Romans 1 tell us exactly the path that those desires will carve in our lives?

> And because they did not think it worthwhile to acknowledge God, God delivered them over to a corrupt mind so that they do what is not right. They are filled with all unrighteousness, evil, greed, and wickedness. They are full of envy, murder, quarrels, deceit, and malice. They are gossips, slanderers, God-haters, arrogant, proud, boastful, inventors of evil, disobedient to parents, senseless, untrustworthy, unloving, and unmerciful. Although they know God's just sentence— that those who practice such things deserve to

die—they not only do them, but even applaud others who practice them. (Rom. 1:28–32)

So it seems this popular message puts us at a dead end, wouldn't you say? If everyone just shakes off the bad feelings that come with doing wrong, society will become utter chaos. And regardless of society, trying to act like you don't feel shame in the presence of a holy God isn't going to work because your conscience will constantly tell you otherwise. As it turns out, "shake it off" is a false gospel because it doesn't hand you anything strong enough to *remove* the shame you genuinely and deeply feel—it just belittles the bad feeling and tells you not to feel it.

Does this mean, then, that we should embrace the opposite message about shame? Instead of casting it off wholesale, should we heap it on? And if there's no way to avoid shame in the presence of God, how do we remove it then? Should we *work* it off?

Good questions. Let's take a look at what happens when we swing the opposite direction, and see if it works out.

Message #2: Work It Off

In one corner, we have those proclaiming the gospel of shamelessness, its core message being "no matter where it shows up, shake it off!" In another corner, we have folks peddling a gospel in the opposite direction. It's a message that might *sound* like it's freeing people from their burdens, but underneath, it actually motivates listeners with—ironically enough—shame. Instead of throwing off shame, this message heaps it on in hopes that the pressure will persuade the listener to hustle harder and eventually work off the bad feelings with good behavior.

Motivational speakers come in all shapes, sizes, and styles. Some people want to be coddled: "Girl, you are a perfect, beautiful butterfly, just *waiting* to sprout her wings!"

Others want their teachers to be relatable: "Hey, boss babe, hey! I see you over there worried about taking the first step. Take my hand. We'll make it together."

But listeners of this gospel message? They want a drill instructor. Think Napoleon Dynamite in the movie by the same name, "Tina, you fat lard, *eat the food*!"

Or, in the case of a lot of modern gurus, *stop* eating the food. Get up off the couch and exercise. Start that business you've always dreamed of. Tell your boss what you *really* think of him. Stop being lazy! Stop being a coward! Don't you see that the only thing standing between you and your dreams is . . . *you*? Be better. Do better. Pull yourself up by your bootstraps and win at life!

Have you ever heard a "motivational" speech that relied on shame to get its point across? Did that work for you? Did you feel empowered to take the reins of your own life, get out of your own way, and conquer?

Many people do. Just like the gospel of *shake it off*, the gospel of *work it off* appeals to a particular audience. Yes, laying the shame on thick can be a little insulting, and yes, it can be a little demeaning, but sometimes . . . that works! Sometimes, it's just the kick in the pants we need to do better and be the best version of ourselves, right?

The logic of this message around shame goes like this: "Hey girl, those bad feelings? You shouldn't cast them off and act like they aren't there. They are there for a reason—they are pointing you to the reality that you're not where you need to be! So the way to get the bad feelings to go away is to find where you've failed and to work really hard to get the guilt off because, girl, *you're a mess!* If you feel mom-shamed, it's probably because you've failed at motherhood in some way . . . so you should get better at it with this eighteen-step plan! If you feel fat-shamed, it's because, sis, *you're just not looking great*—so you should eat less than 1,000 calories a day and you should also get on the treadmill every single day until you see 500 calories have been melted off your lazy behind! The reason you feel ashamed is because you should be—you've transgressed the cultural rules around womanhood, motherhood, and beauty. Work hard enough, reach those goals, check those boxes, do all the things you *should* be doing, and the bad feelings will go away! You'll pay your debt off for breaching the laws, and then you'll feel awesome!"

In this message, instead of no boundaries or standards, there are an infinite number of them, and, at every turn throughout your day, you are brought face-to-face with your failure to attain them. And then you're given a bunch of steps and tricks and hacks and rules to try *yet another time* to hit the ever-elusive mark of success. This "gospel" just doesn't work at removing shame; it only generates more of it. Ultimately, it's a gospel of shaming, or as I like to say, a gospel of "should."

Remember the Cool Girl? She was all about this gospel of shaming. Her favorite word was *should*. I *should* be a content home-maker who doesn't also enjoy other types of meaningful work. I *should* be the perfect mother, who never got to capacity with the number of children she carried and bore. I *should* be the perfect sex goddess, fulfilling my husband's every whim in bed, rain or shine, sick or healthy. (Or on the other side of the spectrum, I *should* be the baddest girl boss in town, and I *should* not *ever* desire to be tied down to married or domestic life!)

When I stared writing about the shame of the "should," I was often met with people who preached the gospel of shaming. The first time I wrote about the Cool Girl, a man commented that he didn't see what was so bad about this woman (who I clearly described as stuffing down her feelings to make her husband happy and not needing anyone, even Jesus): "I'm married to a cool girl and I'm really happy."

Shaming really does seem to work—especially when we're talking about forcing women into certain molds.

- "I feel really bad when my son screams for me in the drop-off line at school. He does it every single day and it breaks my heart. I'm so ashamed. I feel like I should be with him 24/7," one mom says.

- And another responds, "I used to feel the same way. But then I realized that I was *wrong* to drop him off at school. I was supposed to be homeschooling him. That's why it feels bad. You're not supposed to send your son to school."

- Another woman says, "I feel really bad when my boyfriend makes comments about my weight. It makes me feel worthless, and like he'd love me more if I were skinnier."

- Yet another responds, "He probably would. Listen, if you're not working on his ideal body type, he'll find a woman that is. Work out more, and that feeling will go away."

- "I'm so exhausted with my singleness," says one woman. "Sometimes I wonder if it's my fault that I'm not in a relationship yet."
- "It probably is," says another. "If you worked more on yourself/did these ten easy steps/followed this never-fail relationship advice/just stopped looking, you'd be married by the end of the year."

The problem here is that while all of these women *feel bad* about something, the truth is that what they feel is *shame*—not guilt. Why not guilt? Because there is no clear biblical precept that they are transgressing. Are some moms meant to homeschool? Absolutely. But separation anxiety is also completely developmentally normal and, likely, your child will stop screaming at drop-off once he gets more used to school.

Is your worth determined by how thin you are? Of course not. Health is not determined by body size, nor is it healthy for your boyfriend or husband to criticize your body. Do you want to work out more to boost your energy and stay healthy? Get it, girl—taking care of your body is a godly thing to do. But if you hop on a treadmill to keep a man you will never stop running.

Is singleness a by-product of sin? Could be. More likely? It's the calling God has placed on your life, either for a season or for the duration (1 Cor. 7). Marriage is not a reward given to the deserving (or the especially cunning and conniving).

But if we remove the gospel of shaming from these scenarios, then we must acknowledge that sometimes, that shameful feeling isn't a moral guide at all, but an oppressive burden. And also? Sometimes, shame is a liar.

Sometimes, we feel shame when we sin. And that's because we've legitimately done something wrong in the eyes of God's law, requiring us to come out into the light and deal with where we've crossed the line. But other times, we feel shame when no sin is present. This is because we think we've transgressed some "biblical" boundary, but the truth is that the boundary isn't even real in God's Word. It's either culturally contrived or simply imaginary. *Yet we still feel the emotional aftermath of transgressing said boundary because we genuinely thought it was real.*

What does all this tell us? It tells us that the mere presence of shame is not always a reliable indicator of guilt. It means we cannot trust shame to tell us the truth about ourselves, the truth about the law, or the truth about Jesus.

Because while shame is sometimes a truth-teller of a line crossed, it is other times a big fat liar.

And how on earth are we to know the difference? Stay with me—we'll get there.

Ultimately, for now, what you need to know is this: the message of "should" won't work because shame can't be removed by pouring on more of it, nor by trying to work it off.

Message #3: Pass It Off

There's a third message that seeks to declare that shame can be removed by casting it off your own shoulders . . . and onto someone else's. The logic goes like this: *If you have the bad feelings, it's okay; somebody else has them worse than you because they are the truly terrible people. At least you're not them! If you want to talk about people who deserve shame, it's those women!*

I'm sure you witness examples of this all over the place:

- "Okay, mama friend, yes, you're having a hard time nursing that baby around the clock . . . but at least you're not feeding him formula. You're doing so much better for him than that other mom."
- "Yes, marriage is sometimes drudgery, and your husband isn't always Prince Charming. But at least your man isn't an adulterer."
- "Okay, sure singleness and abstinence is hard, but at least you're not a filthy fornicator who is going to hell."

Do you see how this approach shuffles shame off to someone else? How it passes shame off to the next person?

Kind of like when Adam passes his sin on Eve, or when Eve passes it on to the serpent.

Or when Aaron passes his sin off to the people of Israel, and then claims that the golden calf just sprung up out of the fire all by itself (Exod. 32:22–24).

The art of deflection is strong with this one.

Be honest. Have you ever felt shame creeping into your heart and silenced it by focusing on how you're better than someone else?

Remember the story Jesus told about the Pharisee and the tax collector? It helps us see that the strategy of passing our shame down the line fails at removing it:

He also told this parable to some who trusted in
themselves that they were righteous and looked
down on everyone else: "Two men went up to the
temple to pray, one a Pharisee and the other a tax
collector. The Pharisee was standing and praying
like this about himself: 'God, I thank you that I'm
not like other people—greedy, unrighteous, adul-
terers, or even like this tax collector. I fast twice a
week; I give a tenth of everything I get.'

But the tax collector, standing far off, would
not even raise his eyes to heaven but kept striking
his chest and saying, 'God, have mercy on me, a sinner!' I tell you, this one went down to his house justified rather than the other, because everyone who
exalts himself will be humbled, but the one who
humbles himself will be exalted." (Luke 18:9–14)

Sometimes, the only way we know how to squash shame in
our lives is to exalt ourselves over other people. We strive, not for
holiness, but for "betterness." It would be like if Isaiah stood in the
throne room and said, "Okay, so, yes, I am a man of unclean lips,
but have you *seen* that other guy's lips?"

The Pharisee was used to measuring his righteousness by
the unrighteousness (perceived or otherwise) of others. And it is
because of this very attitude that Jesus's most shame-filled words
were aimed right at the heart of the Pharisees, whom he called
"whitewashed tombs" (Matt. 23:27). These men could not humble
themselves in shamefacedness before a holy God because they were
too busy fixating on the perception of their own holiness. In the
end, their strategy of shuffling off their shame didn't come through

for them. It couldn't remove their shame. As Jesus points out, their attempt at deflection leaves them totally exposed and wholly unjustified before a holy God.

It can be easy to read the Bible and mock the Pharisees for their blindness, but have you ever struggled in the same way? Have you ever squirmed at the shame that creeps into your own life . . . until you fixated on someone else's comparative shamefulness? As if we're on a reality show and heaven is a competition to see who can be the *least sinful* instead of the *most righteous?*

"Sure, wifehood and motherhood are hard, but at least I'm in a traditional Christian marriage and I'm not some *idolater*."

"Okay, yes, my political position is fraught with contradictions, but its not as contradictory as *the other side*."

"All right, so I feel bad about this, but at least I feel bad—that other woman is shameless!"

And thus, my friends, we come full circle.

So . . . What Do We Do with the Shame?

If you've made it this far, I'm sure you're wondering what I suggest we do with the shame. After all, the message of "shake it off entirely" won't work with shame. We can't just destroy it altogether. Obviously, it has a place in society and creation. And the message of "work it off by trying harder" won't help us either. We can't use it to motivate us because shame won't always tell us the truth about whether or not we've actually crossed a biblical line. (Even if it could, simply working harder won't get the shame off anyway.) And the message of "pass it off" leaves us sorely lacking as well. We can't shift the blame onto someone else, because when we stand before God, we will stand there alone—not alongside the people we perceive ourselves as "better than."

And so we're left with a bit of a problem, aren't we? This is the third big problem with shame. As we've seen in past chapters, shame leaves us needing a *better covering* (those fig leaves just aren't holding up!) and a *better image* to be conformed into (the Cool Girl isn't real!). Added on top of that, now we see it leaves us needing a *better message* than the various "gospels" swirling all around us (none of them actually *remove* shame the right way). In every way, we need a better solution for the problem of shame than what the world can offer us.

If we take another look at Luke 18:9–14, we see Jesus hinting at what this solution might be.

After the Pharisee finishes his "I'm the best" diatribe, the tax collector speaks:

> "But the tax collector, standing far off, would not even raise his eyes to heaven but kept striking his chest and saying, 'God, have mercy on me, a sinner!' I tell you, this one went down to his house justified rather than the other, because everyone who exalts himself will be humbled, but the one who humbles himself will be exalted." (Luke 18:13–14)

This passage hints toward something that *I can't wait* to unpack with you. Because all three of these shame-answers have something in common. Other than being subpar methods of dealing with the problem of shame, these three "gospels" bypass the truth of the actual gospel altogether.

What does the Good News have to say about our shame? How should believers relate to shame? Will it look differently than the way that unbelievers do? Will we turn down the shame-dial to a quiet hum . . . or is there an "off" switch that will still allow us to pursue righteousness? When the gospels of Shake It Off, Work It Off, and Pass It Off have been rooted out of our lives and supplanted with the gospel of Jesus . . . where will shame find itself? Will it still have a place in our lives?

Friend, you are asking all the right questions. And praise God for the truth of his Word, which stands ready to provide an answer. I am so excited to dig into those answers with you, and to turn our focus from the world's subpar responses to shame to the final Word on the matter.

PART 2

The End of Shame

CHAPTER 4

A Better Covering

I am not a fan of fireworks.

In general, I'm a cautious person. I watch carefully when champagne corks are being popped. I watch the safety demonstration on the airplane just in case there's an emergency and I need a refresher. When I'm going on a kiddie ride at Disney World and they say, "Keep your hands and feet inside of the moving tram at all times," guess whose hands and feet stay firmly within the boundary line? This girl's.

So, I have a general distaste of fireworks, because as beautiful as they are from a distance, up close, I have imagined all the ways that the gorgeous explosion that paints the sky could become life-threatening on the ground.

Yes, I am the life of every New Year's party.

As the year 2017 dawned, I was in Lusaka, Zambia, with my husband, our eight-month-old firstborn, and my very large family of origin. I am the oldest of nine siblings, and most of them are still minors at the time of writing this paragraph. They were ecstatic to have their big sister in town for New Year's Eve, and *so pumped* about shooting off those fireworks.

Now, I couldn't let their big, married, given-birth-to-an-actual-baby sister show that she was terrified to be outside under the night sky with no protection from an errant firework. My fear of a resultant missing eye, finger, or toe couldn't compete with my desire to give my siblings the good time they wanted. So I sat on the balcony of their African home and steeled myself, forcing a smile and executing only marginally convincing *oohs* and *ahhs*.

Only after we had been outside for several minutes did we notice that one of my siblings was missing. I quickly volunteered to find him, because it meant going inside, away from the snap, crackle, and pop that I responded to like a scarred veteran.

I only had to call my brother's name twice before a closet door slid open, and his little frame peeked out from behind it. And I have never felt more understood.

This little boy was terrified of those fireworks. He needed a place to hide.

He needed a covering.

Eve's Predicament and Ours

Adam and Eve would also relate to the frightened child who cowered in that closet physically—just like they would understand the way that his big sister cowered inwardly. Because as soon as they ate the fruit, and shame came flooding into the world, they had a spiritual problem and a physical problem.

Spiritually, though they once only beheld good, their eyes were now *wide open* to evil. They saw their unholiness in the face of God's holiness and *knew*—for the first time, and in a visceral, painful way—that they were unworthy to stand before him. They saw their sin contrasted against his righteousness. They saw their disobedience contrasted against his unwavering standard. They saw their spiritual nakedness in the face of *the Spirit*.

Not only did they see their spiritual nakedness; they saw their physical nakedness too. They went from being naked and unashamed (Gen. 2:25) to hiding behind fig leaves (Gen. 3:7). Then, when they heard God coming, they ducked among the foliage, using the fig leaves to camouflage their physical existence from the God whose vision pierces straight to the heart (1 Sam. 16:7).

It's hard to find an analogy for hiding from a God who is *literally* omnipresent and omniscient. But let's say that my worst nightmares came true, and while I was out on the veranda, an errant firework exploded six feet away from me. Let's imagine I could hold up a fig leaf in front of my face to protect myself from spraying sparks.

Who would be safer? Me, with my fig leaf umbrella? Or my little brother, tucked several more feet away in the closet?

God didn't choose to burn their fig leaves to a crisp, though. Instead, as we've explored before, he asked a question that we *know* he knew the answer to—because he knows all things: "Where are you?" (Gen. 3:9).

And Adam, though afraid, speaks up: "I heard you in the garden, and I was afraid because I was naked, so I hid" (v. 10).

God chooses his response. It isn't, "Why are you afraid?" He knows exactly why Adam is afraid. Remember Isaiah standing in the throne room at a complete loss for words, giving only one utterance at first: "Woe" (Isa. 6:5).

This is the God who will appear before Moses in a burning bush. The God who will pass before that same prophet *backward* (Exod. 33:19–23).

> He said, "I will cause all my goodness to pass in front of you, and I will proclaim the name 'the LORD' before you. I will be gracious to whom I will be gracious, and I will have compassion on whom I will have compassion." But he added, "You cannot see my face, for humans cannot see me and live." The LORD said, "Here is a place near me. You are to stand on the rock, and when my glory passes by, I will put you in the crevice of the rock and cover you with my hand until I have passed by. Then I will take my hand away, and you will see my back, but my face will not be seen." (Exod. 33:19–23)

"Humans," says God, "cannot see me and live."

If we are asking *why*, it is because we do not understand the truth that Isaiah proclaimed in his own brush with the fullness of God's glory. Remember Isaiah's revelation from the last chapter?

> Woe is me for I am ruined
> because I am a man of unclean lips
> and live among a people of unclean lips,
> and because my eyes have seen the King,
> the LORD of Armies. (Isa. 6:5)

So again, God doesn't ask Adam why he's afraid, because God understood the ramifications of eating the fruit before he even uttered the command for Adam and Eve not to do so: the very moment they sinned, they were unworthy to stand in his presence. And *fear* was a proper response to the searing beauty of God's absolute holiness.

He's like turning on a light switch. Every ounce of darkness the light touches *will* be expelled. He's like the noonday heat of the desert. There is no way to escape the burning beams of the sun. He's like being cast into the deepest part of the ocean and searching for air. It's gone.

He is everywhere. And his eyes are upon us at every moment. If we have his favor, this is a very good and beautiful thing. Psalm 139:7–12 says:

> Where can I go to escape your Spirit?
> Where can I flee from your presence?
> If I go up to heaven, you are there;
> if I make my bed in Sheol, you are there.
> If I fly on the wings of the dawn
> and settle down on the western horizon,
> even there your hand will lead me;
> your right hand will hold on to me.
> If I say, "Surely the darkness will hide me,
> and the light around me will be night"—
> even the darkness is not dark to you.
> The night shines like the day;
> darkness and light are alike to you.

This is *great* news when we see God as Father.

It's absolutely crippling news when we see ourselves as fugitives.

Adam and Eve stood before God, knees knocking, bodies quaking, because even though they didn't understand the full gravity of what they had done, shame had given them a whisper of that knowledge—and that whisper was enough to lead them to fear.

But notice that God also doesn't say, "You should be afraid," and then smite them on the spot. No. Instead, he says, "Who told you that you were naked?" (Gen. 3:11). And then, like a loving parent not giving his toddler a chance to lie, continues: "Did you eat from the tree that I commanded you not to eat from?"

And the story spills out.

Yet even as Adam and Eve confess to their sins, they're still trying to use that same camouflage that led them to don fig leaves in a forest.

Camouflaging vs. Covering

> The man replied, "The woman you gave to be with me—she gave me some fruit from the tree, and I ate."
>
> So the LORD God asked the woman, "What have you done?"
>
> And the woman said, "The serpent deceived me, and I ate." (Gen. 3:12–13)

Okay, Adam might have thought. *These fig leaves aren't working at hiding my shame. But what if I hide behind Eve?*

Okay, Eve might have responded. *This man who was singing poetry about me a few verses ago just threw me in front of the bus. Good thing I can blame the serpent.*

And what does God do?

He starts with the serpent and peels back the camouflage one layer at a time. He patiently holds each party accountable for the sin they have committed. Yet before he turns from the serpent to Adam and Eve, in his curse of the serpent he utters the promise that will give their discipline hope. We've looked at this passage once already, but let's look at it again:

> "And I will put enmity
>> between you and the woman,
>> and between your offspring and hers;
> he will crush your head,
>> and you will strike his heel."
> (Gen. 3:15 NIV)

You probably already know this, but in the case you don't, this verse is a big deal. Theologians call it the *proto evangelium*—the first gospel. Why? Because God is telling Adam and Eve some good news by way of a promise. And the promise is this: although there will be ongoing hostility between the serpent (Satan) and mankind, God will ultimately defeat Satan through the seed of a woman— through one of her offspring. One of her descendants—the "someone" we talked about in chapter 1—will crush Satan's head, putting an end to his destruction, deception, and power once and for all. And through this act, mankind has the opportunity to be reconciled to God.

Then, to remind you of something we hinted at in chapter 1, after disciplining Adam and Eve—like the perfect bookend to the *proto evangelium*—God clothes Adam and Eve in animal skins (Gen. 3:21). This clothing will not only offer much more protection from the world that God is sending Adam and Eve into as they leave the garden, it also offers us a beautiful symbol of sacrifice. An animal had to die so that Adam and Eve could be clothed.

Do you see where I'm going here, friend? Have you ever been given cover that you did not deserve? Cover that you did not merit? Has someone ever made a sacrifice for you that changed the course of your life?

If you are a believer, of course the answer is yes. And if you grew up in Sunday school, maybe your inner child is waving their hand with the classic Sunday school answer that is *just right* in this case: "Jesus!"

Jesus is the ultimate covering. Of course he is. Those fig leaves—whatever they are for you—have nothing on the righteous Son of God.

The Better Covering

Instead of letting Adam and Eve stay hidden—forever bound to the shame that confused them—God threw them the ultimate lifeline.

God, in his magnificent kindness, called them out from among the trees and made them a beautiful promise. And he kept that promise with the life of his only begotten Son (John 3:16).

If we trace the lineage through the Bible, the "seed of the woman" turned out to be Mary's Son, conceived by the power of the Holy Spirit, Jesus Christ. The "bruising of his heel" was his crucifixion after living a perfectly blameless life before his Father. The crushing of the serpent's head was the ultimate victory over sin and death that can only be achieved in the person and work of Christ Jesus.

Colossians 1 gives us the opportunity to slow down and savor the story that God has started telling as Adam and Eve stood quaking in their fig leaves in the garden of Eden.

> He is the image of the invisible God,
> the firstborn over all creation.
> For everything was created by him,
> in heaven and on earth,
> the visible and the invisible,
> whether thrones or dominions
> or rulers or authorities—
> all things have been created through him and for
> him. (Col. 1:15–16)

Now, we know that the Son of God has existed for all of eternity. Remember God's words at the very onset of the creation story? "Let *us* make man in *our* image" (Gen. 1:26). John 1:1–5 reiterates this point:

> In the beginning was the Word, and the Word was with God, and the Word was God. He was with God in the beginning. All things were created through him, and apart from him not one thing was created that has been created. In him was life, and that life was the light of men. That light shines in the darkness, and yet the darkness did not overcome it.

If we read further, John 1:14 tells us that this "Word from the beginning" who made the earth at the dawn of time did not stay in the heavens, but instead, "the Word became flesh and dwelt among us." He made the world and then he *entered* it in the person of Jesus Christ.

So, taken all together, Colossians 1:15–16, John 1:1–5, and John 1:14 tell us that: 1) Jesus existed before all of creation, 2) Jesus created all things, both visible and invisible, and 3) all things were made *for his glory*.

So when Adam and Eve sinned, they were not only disobeying God—they were acting *against* the very function for which they were created: to bring glory to the Godhead.

Colossians 1 continues:

> He is before all things,
> and by him all things hold together.
> He is also the head of the body, the church;
> he is the beginning,
> the firstborn from the dead,
> so that he might come to have
> first place in everything. (vv. 17–18)

Adam and Eve's sin separated them from God, but before we even get to talking about the need for reconciliation in verse 20, Paul wants us to know that the need has already been fulfilled. The church is living, breathing evidence of God's faithfulness to sinners. Jesus has already gathered together a people for himself. From the very beginning, we the church were chosen as Christ's inheritance (Eph. 1:18). We—the church—are those whom the Father has given Jesus (John 6:37).

But *how*?

How do we go from standing before a holy God in fig leaves to standing in the throne room completely justified, our shame totally covered with glory?

Jesus is how. Colossians continues:

> For God was pleased to have
> all his fullness dwell in him,

and through him to reconcile
everything to himself,
whether things on earth or things in heaven,
by making peace
through his blood, shed on the cross.
(Col. 1:19–20)

The God of the universe humbled himself "to the point of death—even to death on a cross" (Phil. 2:8) to accomplish the reconciliation that God had promised Adam and Eve back when the world began. He reconciled, not just the people he had called to himself, but the entirety of creation, which is still groaning for his second coming (Rom. 8:22). He made peace through the violence done to his flesh.

He has completely and utterly reconciled us to the Father.

We all stand guilty before a just and holy God. We inherited that guilt from our forefather Adam. But in Christ, we stand before that very same just and holy God *blameless*.

Remember how we talked about the difference between repentance and shame in chapter 1? The difference was this: when sin enters the picture, shame runs *away* from God in fear—it hides. On the other hand, repentance comes out of the shadows and runs *toward* God. Being found in Christ gives you the power to choose the latter. Friend, you can run *to* the Father in confession when you sin, not away from him, because he has already made a profound solution to the problem of your sin by sacrificing his Son Jesus on the cross.

Can you see the good news of the gospel in this? Yes, you'll cross the line sometimes. But all the punishment incurred by your guilt has already been absorbed by Christ. When you sin, yes, you should feel godly sorrow. But you can run to God for help because you have no punishment to fear. There's nothing to keep you in the shadows. The punishment you fear was already poured out on the head of God's Son. All the wrath you're hiding from has already been exhausted. It cannot be poured out on you because Jesus stood in your place and took it on your behalf.

Think about it this way: shame is the emotional aftermath of guilt, right? When you cross a line, guilt is your state of being before God. Remember what we said before? You either *are* guilty or you're *not* guilty in a court of law. And you feel the shame—the embarrassment—of this guilty state when you sin. But if the guilt is paid for—if the verdict in heaven's courtroom is "not guilty" because Christ paid for the sin—then there's no reason to feel the shame associated with the guilt. *Your state of being before God is no longer guilty.* It is, as I said before, *blameless.* And where there's no blame, there's no shame. You don't have to hide anymore because in heaven's eyes, you're not guilty, for Jesus redirected all the wrath for your guilt onto himself. Said another way, you no longer have to feel the emotional aftermath of guilt because the guilt itself is gone.

But shouldn't I feel sorrow when I sin? Yes, we'll get to the good grief of conviction in another chapter. *And isn't God still enormously holy in the moments of my current failures?* Yes to that too. But as believers, we do not have to hide ourselves from the holiness of God, not only because Christ has taken our guilt, but also because of something more—because we have been wrapped in Christ's holiness. What do I mean? I mean that Christ not only paid for our sin, wiping the slate clean in heaven's courtroom, he also filled our record with all his righteous acts. When the eyes of heaven's Judge look upon us, he sees not just "no sin" but also "total righteousness."

A slate not merely empty of wrongdoing, but *filled up* with the very righteousness and holiness of Christ himself! And so, when we come before a holy God, we do not have to balk at his unwavering standard, nor do we have to clothe ourselves in fig leaves because *we have already been clothed in righteousness.* In other words, Christ has made it possible for us to sing along with the hymn writer that we are "dressed in his righteousness alone, faultless to stand before the throne."[5]

If shame is a by-product of guilt, we can repent, meaning, we can turn from the direction we were headed and run straight back to God with *zero* fear, throwing ourselves upon the mercy that God has already displayed to his children time and time again.

Remember, Adam and Eve didn't even have to ask for their fig leaves to be traded for animal skins. God had already made a plan and provision to clothe their nakedness. And, friend, he has already made a plan and a provision to clothe *your* nakedness. And that plan has been executed through the person and work of Christ Jesus.

Friend, do you run toward God or away from him when you sin? Do you stop at the shame—the impulse to hide? Or the impulse to wallow in the embarrassment? Have you allowed that emotion to define you to such a degree that the repentance part never happens? Have you covered yourself in fig leaves or camouflaged yourself in blame-shifting in an attempt to hide the nakedness of your sin from Jesus? Or have you stood bare before him and asked him to clothe you in his righteousness? If you haven't, I'd encourage you to do so right now because your flimsy fig leaves, whatever they are, aren't going to work. There is a better covering you can trust in to hide your shame: Christ's covering of righteousness. His perfect sacrifice—there's nothing else that can take away your blame. His perfect record—there's no better clothing before God to cover your shame.

And if you have trusted in this righteousness, remember this when you sin: *repentance is always the antidote for the shame you feel.* Why? Because by turning toward God when you sin and coming out into the light, you are reminding yourself that strong as shame might try to convince you otherwise, *there's no reason to hide.* You don't have to manufacture some new fig leaf or run back to an old one. You don't have to stay in the shadows, quaking in fear. You are clothed in an imperishable covering that will stand the test of time, and beyond it, into eternity. When you run into God's presence after you sin, you are not running into it exposed. You are running into it *already shielded* from judgment because of Christ's sacrifice for your sin, and *already wrapped*—totally covered—in Christ's holy record. When you stray, and then feel the subsequent shame for straying, you *could* run away from God, because you don't really believe him when he says that the sacrifice of his Son was enough to cover your guilt and put an end to your shame. *Or* . . . you could just run back into God's presence and confess what happened, revealing you truly believe the good news of the gospel, which tells you that where the threat of wrath once awaited you, now there is only mercy, aid, and warmth from your Father to help you change. Dear friend, I urge you to do the latter. To believe the gospel. Because in Christ, you always can run into the presence of God and *you will never be cast out.*

What about When Shame Isn't from Sinning?

"Okay," you might be asking, "I understand that repentance is the antidote for shame . . . but what about when I haven't done anything *wrong*?"

We've already talked about how shame is not always the result of actual wrongdoing. The explanation for the shame that plagues us even when we haven't actively sinned lies right there in Romans 8:22—our entire world has been impacted by the sin and shame of Adam and Eve, and creation is *groaning* to be made new by the second coming of Christ Jesus. Until then, we exist in what's called "the already and the not yet."

Yes, Christ has already died for all our sins. But we have not yet seen this fallen world restored into the glory it was built for.

Therefore, sometimes shame creeps up on us simply because we are still living in a warped version of God's good world where shame still exists. She latches onto so many of our decisions, whether big or benign. She sits in judgment of when we get married, if we have children, how we birth those children, how we feed those children, how we spend our days with those children, how we educate those children, if we can have children, if we stay single, if we have a good enough job compared to others, if we should have a job at all, if we are on enough ministry teams at church, if we should be missionaries, if we should . . . the list never ends.

And in sitting in this judgment over our decisions, she threatens a terrifying consequence: being cast out. Because isn't that what we're afraid of? The shame that comes with being on the outside instead of the inside? After all, if we get don't get married or don't have children, we won't be able to sit at the proverbial table with those who did. If we choose a certain feeding method for our child, or decide on a certain career path, we'll be voted off the island of those who disagree with us. Shame makes us feel like not only are we *wrong* for doing something, we don't *belong* anymore.

And yet somehow, amid all of this, shame comes off like a friend. "Sis, are you *really sure* you should be doing that?" she masks herself as conviction. But unlike true conviction, she's a blob of generic misgivings that aren't rooted in the actual Word of God.

I have felt this kind of shame threatening to eat me alive almost my entire life. We will talk about our new identity in the next chapter, but—suffice it to say—the Cool Girl *thrives* off of shame. She had this carefully choreographed identity—this image she was trying to conform herself into—that is based less on the Word of God than on offering sacrifices to the shame-idol in her heart.

Maybe that shame was foisted upon her by her parents, or her church. Maybe it looks like fitting into the perfect Suzy Homemaker role and making June Cleaver look like a lazy slob. Maybe that shame is thrown at her by the world. Maybe it looks like being supermodel thin. Maybe it's thrown at us by another subculture, one that tells us that we have to be absolutely in love with our bodies every moment of every day or we're not being true to ourselves—or one that tells us that our sexual orientation completely defines us, and that questioning a sexual ethic is inherently wrong and shameful—or one that tells us that we should pursue happiness at all costs, and it's embarrassing to serve a God who requires sacrifice.

Friend, what does your shame-voice sound like? What does it tell you that you can't find in the pages of Scripture? Do you counteract those lies with the truth? Or do you silently make concession to the shame that is constantly ruling your heart?

Shame that points to explicit sins against a holy God make sense. As we've discussed in the last section, when we feel this sort of shame, we can run toward Jesus in repentance because he's already dealt with those sins and clothed us in his righteousness. We can run to the Father without fear because we're covered. But what on earth are we supposed to do when shame pops up out of *nowhere* instead of out of our sinful actions?

We still turn to Jesus.

That same old Sunday school answer? Every time?

Yes. Every time. Because that answer never loses its power. The only way to crowd out the voice of shame is to be rooted in Christ Jesus, who not only covers our shame in the places we genuinely crossed the line, but also deeply understands our plight when shame is thrust upon us *for no good reason*.

Have you ever thought about that? Has it ever occurred to you that shame was heaped on Jesus often in his earthly ministry, and every single scenario was one where he did not sin?

In the places you mess up, his sacrifice and his righteous record have covered you. In the places you haven't messed up, but you're being treated as if you are, he can sympathize with you. Whatever shape the shame takes as it's heaped on you, he knows exactly what it feels like. This is why Jesus is still the answer, Sunday after Sunday after Sunday. He fully understands—like no one else can. Consider how the book of Hebrews puts it:

> **He had to be like his brothers and sisters in every way**, so that he could become a merciful and faithful high priest in matters pertaining

to God, to make atonement for the sins of the people. For since he himself has suffered when he was tempted, he is able to help those who are tempted. . . .

Therefore, since we have a great high priest who has passed through the heavens—Jesus the Son of God—let us hold fast to our confession. **For we do not have a high priest who is unable to sympathize with our weaknesses**, but one who has been tempted in every way as we are, yet without sin. Therefore, let us approach the throne of grace with boldness, so that we may **receive mercy and find grace to help us in time of need**. (2:17–18; 4:14–16)

Your Savior underwent the full human experience. Including shame. Especially the kind of dishonor that sometimes comes with *not* doing something wrong! Your Lord is well acquainted with undeserved shame. Being born of an unmarried couple. Called a drunk and a glutton for daring to draw near to society's bottom dwellers. Rejected even in his own hometown. Cast out of many towns, in fact, not for bad things, but for healing people and doing good deeds! And then, ultimately, hung in humiliation, shame, and nakedness on the cross—a fate for a criminal required of the only righteous human who ever lived. He didn't just bear your sin in that moment; he bore your humiliation too. He bore your *shame*—deserved and undeserved.

Jesus gets it. And he tells you to run to his throne for mercy and grace in your time of need. Feel shame rolling in? That qualifies as a time of need. He stands ready to help you.

And you know what? There's more. More than just understanding or sympathizing with your plight when you feel undeserved shame, Jesus intercedes for you. *Right now.* Did you know that? If you keep reading in Hebrews, you'll see it plain as day:

> He is able to save completely those who come to
> God through him, since he always lives to inter-
> cede for them. (Heb. 7:25)

Your Savior sits at the right hand of the Father, right now, praying for you. He covers you with not just his righteousness, but his very own prayers. He is *for* you in every moment. That includes the moments shame is heaped on you for no good reason. He pleads for you in the throne room, and he will never stop until the day you come to be with him in glory.

Take this in: in the places you sense shame over your sins, Jesus covers you with his sacrifice and righteousness. In the places you sense shame for things that are *not* sin, he bears the humiliation in your place and covers you with his intercession.

In every case imaginable, you are fully covered, my friend.

And so the answer to the bad feelings that come with sinning— for shame that is deserved? Turn to Jesus, the One who reminds you that you're not exposed, you're wrapped up in his righteousness. And the answer to undeserved shame? Turn to Jesus, the sympathizer and interceder for your soul. No matter where the shame originates from, the answer is to turn to Jesus, for he *covers our shame.* Every single time.

Adam and Eve's Covering and Ours

These truths aren't just true for you as an individual. They are true for every individual. Did you know you are swept up in a shame-killing story God has been up to for a really long time—one that has all sorts of women in it? Do you know how far back it goes, or far forward it is reaching, or far wide it extends? Let me expand your gaze.

God did not abandon Adam and Eve in the garden with their newly found shame. Instead, he laid out a plan from eternity past— one that would offer them a covering far greater than fig leaves and far more holistic than animal skins.

The entire story of the Old Testament is God keeping his promise and preserving the seed of the woman. Through Seth— through Noah—through Abraham, Isaac, and Jacob—through Judah—through David. Through slavery and captivity—through obedience and idolatry—through acting like the set-apart nation that they were and acting like the heathens that surrounded them.

Through their constant falling away and constant turning back to God.

Through their constant questioning of the promises that he just kept keeping, no matter what.

Through the sins that they committed and the sins that were committed against them, God preserved Israel, not because she deserved to stand in his throne room—she so often just didn't—but because he had made a promise to Adam and Eve to do just that.

As we know, Jesus was the fulfilment of the promise.

And in him, that promise extended far beyond Israel and her folly to include the women who were often considered to be on the outskirts of God's promises.

Through a Moabite woman named Ruth, who slept at the feet of a kinsman redeemer. Through a prostitute named Rahab who decided to aid the ragtag group of Jews whom God had called to have victory over her city. Through Bathsheba, the woman whom the "man after [God's] own heart" David (1 Sam. 13:14) took advantage of and committed murder to procure. Through Tamar, the woman who was left destitute by the men who were supposed to protect her and resorted to trickery so that the man for whom the Lion of the Tribe of Judah was named would do right by her.

God has a history of inviting the foreigners and the "undesirable" into his promise of deliverance. And that tradition lives on in the New Testament, as Jesus comes and breaks down the barriers between Jew and Gentile, slave and Greek, man and woman to reconcile his chosen people to himself (Gal. 3:28).

Friend, this is such good news.

No matter your heritage—no matter your past—no matter your failings—no matter your victories—no matter your short-comings—no matter your triumphs—no matter your status—no matter your sex—God extends the hand of fellowship to you through Jesus. Instead of quaking before him in fig leaves, he offers us the opportunity to be clothed in the righteousness of Christ and welcomed into the family of faith.

> So, then, remember that at one time you were Gentiles in the flesh—called "the uncircumcised" by those called "the circumcised," which is done in the flesh by human hands. At that time you were without Christ, excluded from the citizenship of Israel, and foreigners to the covenants of promise, without hope and without God in the world.

But now in Christ Jesus, you who were far away have been brought near by the blood of Christ. For he is our peace, who made both groups one and tore down the dividing wall of hostility. In his flesh, he made of no effect the law consisting of commands and expressed in regulations, so that he might create in himself one new man from the two, resulting in peace. He did this so that he might reconcile both to God in one body through the cross by which he put the hostility to death. He came and proclaimed the good news of peace to you who were far away and peace to those who were near. For through him we both have access in one Spirit to the Father. So, then, you are no longer foreigners and strangers, but fellow citizens with the saints, and members of God's household, built on the foundation of the apostles and prophets, with Christ Jesus himself as the cornerstone. In him the whole building, being put together, grows into a holy temple in the Lord. In him you are also being built together for God's dwelling in the Spirit. (Eph. 2:11–22)

My friend, in the flesh, there *was* shame. But now, we have been brought near by the blood of Christ (v. 13). He fulfilled every standard so that we might be united in him (v. 15). He puts the dividing wall of hostility to death (v. 16). He turns us from foreigners into citizens (v. 19), from strangers into family. And he invites us into the sweeping plan that he was unfolding all along.

Shame has *no place* in this new covering. It has been taken away by the person and work of Jesus. I've said it and I'll say it again: it is *no more*. It came tumbling down with all of the other things that separated us from the Son of God before his death, burial, and resurrection. It has been defeated.

> "Do not be afraid, for **you will not be put to**
> **shame**;
> don't be humiliated, for you will not be disgraced.
> **For you will forget the shame of your youth**,
> and you will no longer remember
> the disgrace of your widowhood.
> Indeed, your husband is your Maker—
> his name is the LORD of Armies—
> and the Holy One of Israel is your Redeemer;
> he is called the God of the whole earth.
> For the LORD has called you,
> like a wife deserted and wounded in spirit,
> a wife of one's youth when she is rejected,"
> says your God. (Isa. 54:4–6)

Christ covers the shame not only of you as an individual, but of his bride, the church, and promises her that it has been removed, along with all humiliation and disgrace. We, as a people, are now covered in *his* righteousness. We, as a people, are now partakers in *his* standing before a holy God.

We have had the "woe" Isaiah uttered removed, just like the angels promised back in Isaiah 6:7—the iniquity has been removed. Do you remember what was pressed to Isaiah's lips when he stood before God? It was a burning coal—a symbol of purification and atonement in the ancient world. Like a cleansing agent, it wipes away all contamination or uncleanness before God. And so the picture is this: before Isaiah was allowed to open his mouth to carry a prophetic word to God's people, his unclean lips were purified, atoned for, and wiped clean. And so it goes for you—you've been purified through a cleansing agent. All that made you unwelcome is now wiped clean through the blood of Christ.

I hear the "and yet," my friend, and I wrestle with that "and yet" with you. It's the "not yet" in the "already-and-not-yet." Because even though shame *has already been removed* and was removed the moment Christ said, "It is finished" on the cross (John 19:30), we are *not yet* living in paradise and still have to navigate what it means to grapple with shame in this fallen world.

That victorious language is like the benediction leaving church—the moment we all stand united, hands outstretched, receiving the blessing that the pastor is speaking upon us . . . before we go outside and get pummeled by the waiting and watching world. Because this "not yet" world not only wants to hand out flimsy fig leaves for us to hide behind in its attempt to remove shame, it also wants to hand out two other things we've discussed—other identities and other gospel messages than those found in Christ.

We've talked about the first step: finding a better covering in Christ Jesus. Whether we've sinned or we haven't, we don't need the flimsy fig leaves anymore when the shame comes knocking. We have already been clothed in something that cannot wear out.

And now, as we turn to the second step, finding a better image to be conformed into, keep that Sunday school answer handy in your back pocket. Because that's found in Jesus too.

CHAPTER 5

A Better Image

My hope chest sits in the corner of my bedroom.

Now, unless you're Amish or grew up in my evangelical subculture, the hope chest vibe might not be one that you're familiar with. It's a big cedar chest that my parents gave me when I graduated high school. Proverbs 31 is etched onto the front of it. And inside, I put all of the things that I wanted to take into my future marriage. There are rare books, gorgeous handmade dolls for the fictitious daughter I never had, aprons, children's books . . .

In the middle of this hope chest, there is a box full of pink notebook paper. Lists of my favorite baby names, short stories, and even a retelling of an Arthurian legend adorn those pink pages. And poetry. There is so much poetry.

There are romantic poems—silly poems—poems about identity. But two poems in particular drove me to open that cedar chest and dig into my box as I wrote this chapter. One is called "Trapped," and it's all about being trapped beneath the expectations of others. And the other is called "The Playwright."

In the beautiful cursive of a middle school homeschooler, it begins:

> *Because she is an actor and a playwright, she is always acting out a play.*

And it ends:

> *But she can't stay on stage forever.*
> *The lights will dim.*
> *The audience will leave.*
> *The curtain will fall.*
> *And she will be left holding the mask.*

I was fourteen years old when I wrote those words. I returned to them again at sixteen, eighteen, and twenty. I felt them more and more deeply every time I read them.

Looking back through those poems, it's a wonder that I wasn't diagnosed with depression long before my perinatal anxiety sent me to my first appointment with a therapist. But I blamed my melancholy on a flair for the dramatic—a penchant for navel-gazing. If you had asked me if I was being slowly crushed under the pressure of trying to live up to extrabiblical standards of femininity, I would have told you to take a long walk off a short pier.

The Wrong Image

Growing up in Sunday school in the Bible Belt, Romans 12:1–2 (NIV) is a passage I returned to often:

> Therefore, I urge you, brothers and sisters, in view of God's mercy, to offer your bodies as a living

sacrifice, holy and pleasing to God—this is your true and proper worship. Do not conform to the pattern of this world, but be transformed by the renewing of your mind. Then you will be able to test and approve what God's will is—his good, pleasing and perfect will.

Sunday school teachers, youth leaders, and mentors have stood in front of me to wax eloquent about standing out from the culture around me. Romans 12:1–2 meant not being conformed into the image of the world, and instead being set apart for God like the perfect, blameless sacrifices that his people used to offer him. (We'll talk more about those in the next chapter.)

My parents were first-generation Christians trying to build a safe and loving household for their children out of the wreckages of generational trauma from which they were still healing. I can only imagine what it felt like to try to figure out how they would teach us to navigate the world around us when they themselves did not have much of a model for navigation sitting in front of them. Perhaps that's why Paul instructed the Corinthians to imitate him as he imitated Christ (1 Cor. 11:1)—earthly models can be so helpful.

My parents, like many Christian parents, were in search of those earthly models. They made decisions to protect me from being conformed into the image of the world, and I was *ready* to resist its alluring call, which, in my circles at the time, meant being able to argue against secular humanism, evolution, or certain methods of child-rearing.

What I was *not* ready for was the fact that being conformed to the image of the *world* wasn't the only thing holding me back from being transformed.

Turns out, as we explored in chapter 2, there was this whole other image calling out to me too, beckoning me to become more and more like her.

We know her well by now. The Cool Girl.

She was the mold I was supposed to run toward when I ran away from the image of the world. She was the model, the pattern, of what I was supposed to become instead of patterning myself after the surrounding culture. As I put off the world, she was the persona I was supposed to put on.

And as I look back, I can now see that what it meant to be her was mostly oppositional. I could tell you who I *wasn't* supposed to be much more easily than I could tell you who I *was* supposed to be. I could argue with you all day long about a woman's place. But if you asked me to paint a picture of womanhood that relied not on overblown caricatures of the cultural norms, but on purely biblical love and excitement for who and how God had made me . . .

I would be lost.

As much as it looked like I was getting it right, I was mostly getting really good at the *appearance* of being right with God. When it came to outward shows of the Cool Girl, I was the best. But who I really was on the inside? She was less centered on Jesus than she was on quieting the constant din of shame that told her she wasn't quite good enough.

A Better Image

If we recall from chapter 2, running toward the image of the Cool Girl as a way of escape from the image of the world was never going to work. Why?

Because the Cool Girl isn't real, because the Cool Girl is a mixture of ungodly and godly elements, and because becoming like her is a process you can't ever complete—meaning, forming myself into the image of the Cool Girl was never an attainable goal anyway.

A conundrum naturally arises in my story here.

If I was dead set on *not* conforming to the image of the world, but I was mistaken to conform instead to the image of the Cool Girl, was there a better image to run toward instead? And what image, exactly, should I have run toward?

I must be the world's worst Sunday schooler because it took me too many years to realize the obvious answer Scripture had been holding out in front of me all along.

Consider Romans 8:29:

> For those [God] foreknew he also predestined to be **conformed to the image of his Son** . . .

Or how about Colossians 3:10?

> . . . You are being renewed in knowledge **according to the image of your Creator.**

As it turns out, I was never made to fit the mold of some immaculately polished starlet or superwoman. I was made to fit the mold of my Savior and Creator. And the same is true for you. You were not made to be conformed into the image of this world, nor the image of the cultural Cool Girl, however she is defined in your circles. You were destined to be conformed into a better image, dear reader: the image of Jesus Christ.

Getting Image Right

"Alright," you may be saying to yourself, "I get your train of thought. But what *is* the image of Christ, exactly?"

Let's start with the beautiful truth of who Christ really is, which can be found throughout Scripture. Christ is "the image of the invisible God, the firstborn of all creation" (Col. 1:15 ESV). He is "the radiance of the glory of God and the exact imprint of his nature" (Heb. 1:3 ESV). He is the perfect image of God because he *is* God wrapped in flesh. Meaning, if we want a living, breathing, touchable way to see God in visible form, Christ is it. As one commentator would put it, to say "Jesus is God's image" is to say Jesus is "the visible form of the invisible God."[6]

If we want a perfect image to run toward in this life, an ideal silhouette out on the horizon of our future that we might become more like, why would we ever think the Cool Girl could compete with the Son of God?

After all, he is who we were made to image from the beginning, before the fall.

See, the Son of God is the Second Person of the Trinity, and the Second Person of the Trinity was there—along with God the Father and God the Spirit—at the dawn of creation. The Son of God was one of the persons present when that famous decree rang out from the heavens: "Let *us* make man in *our* image" (Gen. 1:26).

And so Adam—and all of mankind after him—was made according to God's decree.

But upon the fall, Adam—and all of mankind after him—failed to properly reflect the Creator in whose image he was made. The reflection was recognizable, but marred and distorted, like a shattered mirror that shows evidence of what a person is *sort of* supposed to look like, but the picture is in a million pieces that clearly doesn't reveal a unified whole.

And so, it seems, the world needed a new Adam—a Second Adam—who could come and succeed where the first one failed when it came to perfectly imaging God.

As Romans 5 tells us, a Second Adam came, indeed. And he succeeded in every place his predecessor failed. As we know, his name is Jesus Christ. And as I said before, he's the *perfect* image of God because, unlike the first Adam, Jesus *is* God.

Here's the relieving news for you in this: there's a reason you have a deep longing to arrive at some better version of yourself. There's a reason you reach for some picture-perfect icon to pattern yourself after. There's a reason you feel a profound instinct to be shaped into some sort of ideal—to move forward, to get better, to grow. And that's because you were originally made to exist in a faultless state, completely conformed into the perfect ideal. And so it makes a lot of sense that there's this nagging voice in the back of your head that tells you that you aren't there yet—you haven't reached conformity to such a state. That voice is telling you the truth. There *is* a perfected version of you out there on the horizon, and you *haven't* made it there yet.

The problem is not that you desire such a perfect state, dear reader, or that you sense deep in your bones that you haven't arrived at it yet. Rather, the problem is that the image to which you chose to conform yourself was the wrong one. You, like me, probably tried to better yourself by running toward the image of the Cool Girl, but she couldn't help you get to where you want to go. She's not the right image to run toward because she isn't faultless, and she does not perfectly or fully image God. She was never the perfect human who reflects God in all the ways a human should. *Jesus* is. And if you try to substitute some other figure in his place, if you try to pattern yourself after any other mold, you'll never feel like you're actually getting anywhere. For he is the very God you were made to image all along. He's the icon. He's the silhouette. He's the ideal of what it truly means to be human.

And if Christ is the very God we were made to image, then becoming more like him does more than make us better over time—it actually takes us back to that "pre-shame" place that Adam and Eve experienced in Eden.

Remember how the Bible says "both the man and his wife were naked, yet felt no shame" before God (Gen. 2:25)? That's because, at that part in their journey, they were in their original, faultless state, perfectly imaging God just as they were supposed to. *This is the state you and I crave to be in every moment of every day.* We want it back. And patterning our lives after Jesus is the only way to get us there.

As we become more like the One who perfectly images God, we feel the load of shame lighten. Said another way, the Bible says we are slowly being made into the image of Christ, which means we're slowly being restored back into the image that was shattered and distorted by the fall back in Genesis. *Becoming like Christ helps us become who we were always supposed to be before sin and shame entered the picture*—it forms us back into the shape we were always meant to take. A shape that knows nothing of shame and the isolation it brings—only pure and uninhibited intimacy with the One who created us.

Dear reader, Christ didn't just cover your shame and then leave; he gave you the perfect image to become more and more like over time. As you put off the world, he gives you a perfect persona to put back on. He *restores* you to the pre-shame relationship with the Father so that you can live a life of fullness as his child.

How to Transform

As we've said, we were made to be conformed to the image of God (Rom. 8:29). The natural next question is how. Thankfully, God gives us a road map of exactly what that looks like.

The Bible says we conform into Jesus's image in two ways: one, we "put off" the old self—the one patterned after the world. And two, we "put on" the new self, which is patterned after Christ (Col. 3:9–11; Eph. 4:24). We change clothes.

This act of "changing clothes" means we have been saved, not just to sit in a corner and wait for glorification to come to us, but to *participate* in the good works that Christ has set before us (Eph. 2:8–10). Said another way, when God looks at us, he indeed sees us covered in Christ's righteousness—in Christ's clothes. Those clothes were a gift to us. And now our job is to *walk* in them. We were saved not just to know Christ, but to emulate Christ as we grow in the fruit of his Spirit—in love, joy, peace, patience, kindness, goodness, gentleness, and self-control (Gal. 5:22–25). We were saved to flee from the deeds of the flesh that sow an inheritance of shame and separation from God: sensuality, idolatry, sorcery, enmity, strife, jealousy, fits of anger, rivalries, dissensions, divisions, envy, drunkenness, orgies, and things like these.

We have been saved from the shame that crouches outside of our door ready to consume us at the slightest provocation.

His image is the only one that offers us a new beginning—a beginning like the one our first parents forfeited when they ate the fruit.

Okay. That's it. Put the book down and walk away because the answer to shame is clear as day: just be like Jesus. Simple, right?

If only.

The True Image and You

Here's the thing: you likely picked up this book knowing a few Sunday school answers. Maybe you already knew back in chapter 2 that young Jasmine needed to trade the image of the Cool Girl for a better one—Christ. Because only hidden in him could she find true contentment and a reprieve from shame and live happily ever after.

That sounds really great, Jasmine, but how on earth am I supposed to parse out the difference between the false image and the real one?

That's a good question, especially when the false image isn't all bad, or when it's so deeply entrenched in you that you can't see out of it.

Remember, friend, your Cool Girl might not look exactly like mine did. Maybe your story is the foil of mine. Maybe you grew up in an environment that prized education and a high-paying job— you know, the life where Monday mornings look like you heading off to the downtown high-rise in your power suit, and the husband and kids are either nonexistent or tucked somewhere in the background. And maybe in this sort of environment, to have any desire outside of that picture was unheard of. Maybe you kept it a secret that you wanted to be a wife and stay-at-home mom with a gaggle of children. Maybe you felt ashamed to acknowledge such a desire because you feared that those around you wouldn't see it as enough of an achievement. Or, maybe your hometown considered educated people too "elite," and so you never had the courage to communicate that really, what you deeply wanted was to continue your education and pursue an advanced degree.

Or maybe your identity wasn't shaped by a subculture as much as it was a certain man (or set of men)—by what you thought they wanted, and who you thought they wanted you to be. Maybe it's been shaped by your mother, and her aspirations for your future that had more to do with her living through you than her loving you well. Maybe it's been shaped by your father, who didn't stick around long enough to speak life into you, but whose absence spoke all the death it possibly could in life's stead. Maybe it's been shaped by your best friend—your boyfriend—your mentor—your pastor—your boss.

And maybe every time you try to figure out *who you are* apart from the cacophony of voices that has always been so eager to tell you, all you hear is . . .

Not silence.

Shame isn't silence.

It's more like static in a long-distance phone call, or a glitchy screen during FaceTime with your friend. The conversation is happening, but you can't access it because the reception is just . . . off.

Have you been there? Have you felt like who God was calling you to be—not just "like Christ" in a general, nebulous way, but "what *I* look like as I emulate Christ"—is *right beneath the surface* of that heavy film of shame? Have you been unsure of how to wipe away the smudges on the mirror to see the reflection that you feel is *fighting* to look back at you?

Me too.

I've imagined the girl in the mirror in so many ways. Sometimes, she looks exactly like the girl that shame told me was the only version of me that my peers would accept: the quiet, docile, plastic, ever-serving, never-struggling, rarely *thinking* stay-at-home mom (and sex goddess) in whom her husband always delights. Sometimes, in moments of complete and utter rebellion, she looks exactly like the girl shame told me I could never be: a loud, domineering, calculating career woman whose husband better get in line behind her email in-box.

Notice how both women are complete caricatures?

That's what shame does. It presents you with two equally vapid options, promising you that there is safety in the lack of nuance. And so helpful questions to ask yourself as you parse out your own Cool Girl are: *What two extremes or "profiles" do I find myself bouncing between, and are either of them the profile of Christ? Do either of them allow me to be a human or do they require me to be an impossible standard of superwoman?*

After reflection, you'll be able to sketch out who your Cool Girl is over against the real you, with all her limitations and shortcomings and complicated issues. And then, if you're anything like me, with the mold of the Cool Girl pulled off of you and the "real you" now exposed and vulnerable, this will be the point in your journey where you're left wondering what in the world it could possibly look like for *you*, a *woman*, in all your complexity and personality traits and life-situations and gifts and idiosyncrasies to successfully "put on Christ." After all, the Cool Girl wasn't actually the standard of perfection, but Jesus *is*. If you couldn't hack it as the imperfect Cool Girl, how in the world are you going to become more like perfection itself?

The image of Christ is great as a concept—but are there any women who show us what it looks like to put on his image while also avoiding the world *and* the masks of cultural caricatures? Who are fully themselves, in all their three-dimensional complexity, *and* who are also like Christ? Who truly become more like him even though they're a mess? And how do they gain the power to do so?

The Attainable Image

John 4:1–42 tells the story of one such woman. It records the Samaritan woman's meeting with Jesus.

The Samaritan woman is going about her daily life, conducting a ritual that any woman of her time could relate to—drawing water. As many thinkers note, women in that day would have gone to draw water during cool parts of the day to avoid the heat, but this woman goes at the hottest part of the day, likely to avoid the disapproving faces of the nearby townspeople. She is used to being ignored, not just by the Jews with whom her people have centuries-long animosity, but likely by most polite society because, as verses 16–18 tell us, she has been married five times and lives with a man who is not her husband. Viewed as an ethnic outsider and likely an adulterer, this is a woman well-acquainted with shame.

And yet, Jesus seeks her out and engages her. He lays bare the shame that she carries and promises her, not only temporary reprieve, but lifelong healing. She knows that the Messiah is coming (v. 25), and though Jesus would sometimes purposefully hide his identity from certain interrogators, Jesus openly reveals himself to her: "I, the one speaking to you, am he" (v. 26).

My shame seems insignificant next to the woman at the well's. Even if I had been divorced *ten* times, I do not live in the same sort of society that would've marginalized me to the extent that this woman was marginalized.

But I've been thirsty too.

Not for the brief reprieve of a few sips of water, but for the well that never runs dry.

I relate so deeply to the Samaritan woman's request: "Sir, give me this water."

Because the water that I've been drinking just leaves me thirsty again and again.

The tirelessly exacting standards of womanhood that our culture throws in my face leave me thirsty again and again.

The failings of evangelical Christendom to truly reflect the heart of our Savior toward women leave me thirsty again and again.

The relentless pursuit of peace outside of Jesus leaves me thirsty again and again.

And I cannot keep coming to the well over and over again, dehydrated from chasing the mirage that is the Cool Girl.

I need to drink deeply from the well that will never run dry.

The Samaritan woman—she did just that. Notice how long her conversation with Jesus lasted: *twenty* verses (vv. 7–26). Far longer than the rich young ruler, and lengthier too than many of his conversations with Pharisees. To her, indeed, was given a long drink from a deep well.

And after this long drink, notice her quick two-verse response in verses 28–29:

> Then the woman left her water jar, went into town, and told the people, "Come, see a man who told me everything I ever did. Could this be the Messiah?"

Dropping her water jar, she forsakes the vessel that she once trusted to quench her thirst, for she had finally found the real thing. And she doesn't stop there. Instead of living a life that looked a lot like that water jar—dry, leaky, cracking, frail, always in need of filling—she takes a different shape. A shape that looks a lot less like the empty vessel at the well and lot more like the man at it. Said another way, after forsaking her other source of water and drinking deeply of Christ, she starts conforming to his image.

How so? By running *toward* those she'd usually keep at great distance. Just as the Son came and got into our world, moved into our neighborhood, and sought us out at great cost to himself, so she does for the nearby townspeople. This time, though, she doesn't care what they think. She isn't ruled by the shame that once kept her at bay. She's found living water, and she runs right into the middle of the snooty, condemning, self-righteous community who needs it just as much as she did. Just as Jesus went out of his way to pursue a woman who did not fit her culture's "laws" of womanhood, nor the biblical standard of it, so now this very woman goes and does likewise. She pursues the Samaritans down the street—those who do not fit the Jewish cultural ideals, nor the biblical ideals, of faithfulness to God's law.

What I love about her story is that she reveals what it could look like to run away from the world's mold (forsaking the water jar for the real thing) and conform to Christ's image instead (moving toward a people who do not deserve it), all *without* suddenly becoming a caricature of what her society expected a woman to look like. She didn't go clean herself up first. She didn't stop to put on a corset and a freshly pressed dress (or in her time, a heavily gold-beaded tunic with a brand-new leather belt to emphasize her waistline). She didn't wait until she had a long-standing marriage and a gaggle of sons walking in her wake before she made a move. She also didn't shake off the community entirely, saying, "So long, shamers! Serves you right for outcasting me like that! I'll take this living water for myself, thank you very much, but you can die of thirst!"

Instead of these extremes, the woman at the well just "put on Christ" right where she was, with all she had, right in the middle of her complicated story. She looked like herself *and* more like Christ at the same time. Becoming more like him—beginning her process of being conformed into his image—was *actually attainable* for her. And it is for you and for me too.

Again, her power to do this came not from taking classes on how to be a Christian, or from checking off the boxes required by the in-crowd (who, by the way, came to faith in droves because of her testimony; vv. 39–42), but from personally drinking deeply from the well that will never run dry.

Dear friend, the point is this: before we get to the *doing* of becoming more like Jesus, we have to understand the *being* of having been rescued by him. We have to understand that he has loved us with a matchless love that led him to die on the cross so that we could be reconciled with his Father in heaven. We have to understand that he has already made a way for us to draw near to God— that he's already lived a life of perfect imaging in our stead.

I don't want you to leave this chapter with the notion that if you can just figure out all of the perfect rules in Scripture, you'll escape from the never-ending cycle of shame. Because you won't. Apart from Jesus, even the most law-abiding woman is still going to struggle with shame.

Because apart from Jesus, shame's discipleship is the only teacher we know.

Don't be like Martha—rushing straight to the doing.

Be like this woman at the well, and also like Mary—and sit at Jesus's feet for a moment first.

Sit at Jesus's feet and soak in the knowledge of *who he is* . . . that's the right one.

It's not oppositional or combative. It's not performative or flashy. It doesn't rush to doing.

It's about sitting. Soaking in. Abiding. It's about enjoying the twenty verses of *engagement* with Jesus before you try to do the two verses of acting like him. For you cannot image someone you have spent no time with.

Have you ever felt that you had to earn God's love? Have you ever found yourself calculating what you might have to do to be seen as acceptable to him? Cherished by him? Have you ever gotten it backward, spending only two verses worth of time drinking from the well himself and twenty's worth trying to pour out from a vessel whose shape is the perfect woman? Has your version of the Cool Girl ever been a game you're playing to try to be acceptable to the Most High God?

Have you been playing the game for so long that you don't even know who you are anymore?

We still have a chance to choose the better portion, friends. The answer to our identity is neither found in navel-gazing, nor in stuffing it all down and trying to work our way into God's favor, nor rushing to put on the mask of some cultural caricature. The answer to our identity is *sitting in the living room*. Or on your bedside table. Or on your bookshelf. Or buried in the junk in your car.

It's the Word of God.

And not just the written Word of God, but the Word become flesh, Christ Jesus.

Shame is a broken compass, beloved. But the Word points true north.

Getting Rid of Shame . . . the Right Way

I'm returning to Eve's story again and again because, truly, in the words of Julie Andrews's Maria von Trapp, it's best to begin at the beginning.

Shame was not the ultimate villain in Eve's story, just as it is not the ultimate villain in ours. This is important to remember, because we live in a culture that is quite vocal about what an enemy shame is, and how we need to do away with it and live in our truth unabashedly before the world!

As a believer, though, it is not ultimately *my truth* I want to bask in before the world, but God's. Even if Eve had never felt the blush of shame about her transgression . . . she was still guilty of a transgression. She was still guilty of disobedience and there needed to be a penalty paid for that disobedience.

This is not language we love, and I get that. We just want to burrow in God's chest and cry out to him with all our shame-hurt and all our shame-pain. And we *can*! But the reason we can is because God fulfilled the promise of Genesis 3:15 by sending his Son Jesus to pay the penalty owed for our sin (1 John 2:2).

This is not a book of doing away with all the bad feelings that accompany being on the wrong side of a boundary that the Lord has set. Were I to write such a book, I would be guilty of leading you astray.

So this is not a chapter about finding your identity in throwing off the fig leaves and frolicking naked through the garden. No, friend, you *need* clothing.

It just needs to be the proper clothing.

It needs to be the righteousness of Christ (Isa. 61:10), not your work and worth as the Cool Girl.

This is a book about putting shame in its proper place: crushed under Jesus's heel, and then, once it's removed, actually having the ability to become more like him.

And so, as I ponder Eve's story alongside the story of the woman in John 4, I naturally think back on my own story—particularly the shame I experienced as I grew into adulthood. And I realize that the answer to becoming the woman God wanted me to be was not to look deep inside of myself and find the power to be an individual, subcultural norms be darned. Said another way, the answer was not to put on the image of the world and just act like biblical boundaries aren't real. For the image of the world is diametrically opposed to the image of God. And yet, nor was the answer to double down on the surrounding subcultural norms and form myself into a caricature of the Cool Girl. For she was not the right image either. She was just a mask.

The answer, instead, was to look to the cross and to find my identity in the finished work of Jesus. He is the truer, better, and total image of God, and his gospel work is the only thing strong enough to remove the shame that comes with diving headlong into the world *and* into false Christian stereotypes.

An Example

We've talked about what this looks like for Eve and for the woman at the well, but what about you and me, right here and right now?

I can't answer that for you, but for me, it has looked like obeying wherever God's Word puts up an actual boundary, and heeding it, lest I fall into the sin that nailed Jesus to the cross. And then, where God has given us freedom, it looks like letting myself actually *be free*.

I'll give you one example to bring this chapter to a close.

Let's consider the unscriptural boundaries that twenty-year-old Jasmine had erected around what it meant to be a woman of God. I had set up an unbiblical dichotomy in my mind between pursuing a career and becoming a mother. I would have argued that working women were trying to find their satisfaction in their careers and callings *outside of the home*, but the real satisfaction came from obeying God through my calling *inside of the home*. You may know the characters in this story well. In this corner, we have the cultural stereotype of a woman who must pursue her goals at all costs—even at the expense of her family. In this corner, we have the evangelical stereotype of a woman who must seek satisfaction at home at all costs—even at the cost of her gifts. And never the twain shall meet.

She can't have it all. She must either be satisfied at work or at home. Those were my options.

But upon inspection, I've noticed that both stereotypes and the peddlers thereof forget that the only *real* satisfaction in her life comes from Jesus.

Of course, you're thinking. But the *of course* there is not as obvious as we sometimes think it is. Because though we verbally assent to the idea that Jesus is supposed to be our all in all, we function in a way that takes him for granted and moves other things to the center.

This can happen at work . . . and at home.

As I've wrestled through Jesus being the deep well from which all believers are supposed to drink (not career, and not family status), which in turn makes us more like him over time, I have concluded that what should satisfy wives is the same thing that should satisfy husbands.

Think about it. If my husband is finding his satisfaction and purpose from his job, his identity is misplaced. And worse than that, if his career is the well from which he drinks deeply, he will inevitably begin to conform to the world—one where men everywhere are being shaped into the image of the workaholic, uninvolved father. On the other hand, if my husband was finding his entire satisfaction in me, his identity would again be misplaced, and he'd still end up being formed into some other image—probably the Cool Guy image, where the worth of a man is measured by the woman on his arm.

For some reason, it's always been easier for me to assent to these truths for husbands, but much harder for wives. *Of course* husbands shouldn't be ultimately satisfied with their jobs or their family status, but somehow, admitting this same biblical truth for wives comes with a litany of caveats.

As an actual wife and mother, ways that I structure my life and my gifts have much less to do with constructing prime personal satisfaction than with satisfying my Maker. Whatever is on my plate during a particular season presents opportunities to grow in my understanding of and willingness to serve the center of my satisfaction: my Savior. This side of heaven, I'll never reach full satisfaction, but glorification awaits me.

I can't tell you if your job is an idol. I can't tell you if your marriage is an idol. I can't tell you if waking up in your right mind or being of sound body is an idol. But I can tell you that your work, your family, your health . . . those are all gifts meant to be stewarded in the service of Almighty God, and they could all be gone tomorrow, and he'd *still* be Almighty God. Being satisfied in him is a constant battle; just ask Job. But it's a battle I am willing to fight.

In my own journey, I've found that I can talk about moms and their priorities, and that's an important conversation. But not before I get this right. Because if I elevate wifehood and motherhood as the primary source of satisfaction in my life, or if I make it the central focus and message for other women who happen to be listening to me, I'm not speaking with biblical priorities any more than the world I claim to be combatting is. Man or woman, married or unmarried, childless or house-full, satisfaction comes from Christ alone, and will only be known perfectly in eternity with him. Full stop. Deep breath. And then I can enter in conversations about everything else.

My Teenage Cool Girl

If I could, I would go back in time and put an arm around teenage poet Jasmine, and I'd tell her what every iteration of the Cool Girl mask misses.

I would tell her what I want you to know: that your identity doesn't have to be shaped by the world, nor does it have to be shaped by the cultural standards of others. That while your desire for the mask makes sense—after all, you, like all of us do, want to take the shape of something perfect—it is not transforming you into who God would have you become. I would say, "You can always take off the mask, Jasmine. At any time. For there's something better to put on, an image far more beautiful and far more attainable."

I'd lead her to that looking glass, and I'd say, "If you're willing to be brave, put down the mask, dear one, and put on Christ, who—if you forsake all other identities and drink deeply from him—will not make you choose between a truer version of yourself and a better one. For in him—in the One who crushed the head of the serpent, in the One who cleaned the mirror, in the One whom all your insecurities are covered—*you get both*. And when your identity is hidden in him, shame can't touch you."

And lastly, I'd remind her, as I'll remind you, about a promise Scripture makes about what shape we will take in the afterlife, when all is said and done. Thankfully, the promise is not that we'll bear resemblance to a Christian superwoman, but rather, to our Savior:

> And just as we have borne the image of the man
> of dust, we will also bear the image of the man of
> heaven. (1 Cor. 15:49)

CHAPTER 6

A Better Message

When I was sixteen years old, I lied to a new friend.

We were sitting on her bed, talking about all the things that sixteen-year-old girls talk about—cute boys, school woes, future aspirations—when her iPod shuffled to a Norah Jones song. My friend grinned and paused, sighed, and said, "I *love* this song! Norah Jones is the best, right?"

And I smiled back at her and said, "Oh my goodness, I *love* Norah Jones."

Reader, I did not love Norah Jones.

In fact, I was on record as having asked my Norah Jones fan of a father to skip the six hundredth playing of "Don't Know Why."

But this was a new friendship, and I really, really wanted her to like me, so I lied. And consequently, every time we were together, she would turn on Norah Jones as a sweet little favor to me. "I know you love her!"

I lied because friendships were hard for me, and I really wanted to gain one in this girl. I lied because she seemed way cooler than

I was, and she knew what kind of music cool girls who wanted friends should listen to. I lied because I was a lonely homeschooler who just really needed a friend, and I didn't want to risk her backing away from me when the chance at a *bona fide* BFF was right at my fingertips.

I lied because I wanted to belong.

The Out Crowd

As I've turned that memory over in my mind, I've realized that grown-ups in today's world aren't all that different from sixteen-year-old Jasmine. We all naturally desire to have a place in some sort of network or community greater than just ourselves. One could even argue that this desire is behind the recent online trends of things like cancel culture, mommy wars, political polarization, and all sorts of shaming. One could argue that each of these are simply equivalents of voting the "bad guys" off the island of "the good guys," whoever "the good guys" seem to be to a certain group of people. To be in the in-crowd, you have to purge others to the out-crowd.

Think about it. When you cancel someone, you're saying, "You don't belong anymore, and I belong with the good people who have a problem with you." When you join in with like-voices (whether they are moms who agree with you on some issue or the political party that best represents your views) as they belittle those who take a different approach, you're saying, "We belong to the community who has it right and you deserve to be not only pushed out of the camp, but publicly humiliated."

Now, ideological differences *certainly* matter, and it's a good thing to make distinctions clear. But it seems that, overall, digital interaction with other human beings these days has been reduced to one big experiment in just how brutally we can cast one another out. All of this because we are teenage Jasmine inside.

We all—every single one of us—desperately want to belong.

Which is why false gospels are so attractive to us. They promise us that if we follow their precepts, we will be given a place in a certain community and we won't ever have to worry about being cast out.

The Promise of Belonging

Think back to the three false gospels that we combatted in chapter 3:

- Shake It Off: shame is something that we should ignore, or throw off of us any time we feel bad feelings, and it will go away
- Work It Off: shame is something that we can off-load by working harder
- Pass It Off: shame is something that we can off-load by putting it on someone else

Not only do all three of these "gospels" come with a false promise to remove shame, all three come with an equally false, built-in promise of community. After all, every gospel comes with its own people group. Let me explain.

With the gospel of "shake it off," you are promised a sense of belonging to the group who tell shame to take a hike—even when they do shameful or hurtful things to others. And the siren's call of that group is appealing for so many reasons. "Come to our camp! You can live however you please, and no one will ever have the right to cancel you! After all, we are the ones who aren't restrained by any negative emotion! Come be part of a community that throws off all cultural restraints of feeling bad about anything! You can be you, no discernment required, along with all of us who agree with that mindset. Free yourself and belong to us!"

Or maybe you are naturally attracted to the people who subscribe to the second message—the ones who work shame off as a self-motivational tool. You like the feeling of belonging to them—after all, they've figured life out in ten clear steps. They bring a sense of completion and certainty to your life as you join arms with their community, which promises if you all just suffer together through the gauntlet of performance long enough, you'll all feel *fantastic* on the other side. And that's appealing. A community that promises *no more guilt* on the other side of some hard work? Who doesn't want that? "Come to our camp! You'll become the best version of yourself because you will so loathe all alternate versions of who you could be!"

Or maybe your people are of the "pass it off" variety, the ones who play the blame game, just like Adam in the garden. This community is appealing too, for it's the tribe who are always a little bit better than the next group in their own eyes. A little bit cleaner of conscience. A little bit purer in heart. And who doesn't want to feel like they are in the community who got the higher grade on the curve? Who wouldn't want to belong to the group who isn't *that* guilty? "Come to our camp! We are so much better than all those other camps! Those other camps are the worst camps in camp history, and even if you're awful, you're still not as bad as those other camps!"

Whatever your false gospel of choice, there is strength in numbers. We were not made to fight the battle of shame alone, and when we turn to these false gospels, we will inevitably find the people of that gospel waiting to welcome us into the fold and tell us that we're not only one step closer to silencing shame for good, but also permanently installed in the camp without fear of having to be shoved outside of it. In short, the messages of the false gospels surrounding us is not only *here's a way to remove shame*, but also *here's a way to belong forever—you'll never been shunned if you stick with us!*

Problem is, as you've probably experienced or witnessed time and time again, false gospels always fail to deliver on both those promises. For reasons we saw in chapter 3, these deceptive narratives utterly fail to *actually* remove shame. And as you've likely seen in the news, on social media, or in your own life, all sorts of communities that once promised a forever-place to belong end up throwing out longtime members at the drop of a hat. Over and over again we see that when it comes to false gospels, the message didn't truly offer good news and the place of belonging was never permanent.

Outside the Camp

Strange as it may sound, the ancient and overlooked book of Leviticus understands these in-crowd/out-crowd dynamics.

But if many of us are honest, Leviticus is one of those books we've been tempted to skip over in our Bible reading plans. It outlines the rules and regulations that governed ancient Israel, from worthy sacrifices to holy days, to civil laws, to how to respond to basic bodily functions. The Bible tells us that Jesus is the fulfilment of the law (Rom. 8:3–4), which is why we do not sacrifice in the

temple when we have sinned—he became the ultimate sacrifice for
us. And if we know that, it can be easy for us to skim Leviticus and
check off the box in our brain: this stuff isn't important, because
Jesus has already taken care of it, and aren't we lucky we don't have
to kill turtledoves when we sin?

Now, don't get me wrong. The ceremonial law of Leviticus—
the laws governing how Israelites related to God before Jesus came
and left the Holy Spirit in his wake—are overwhelming to read,
even when we agree that they no longer apply to us. But if we skip
over them, we miss more than the minute details of Israel's sacrificial system. We miss the depths to which Jesus has taken on our
shame.

As I mentioned, Leviticus outlines strict rules of cleanliness
that have to do not only with sinful behavior, but with bodily functions, as well as disease. Lepers, for instance, had to go "outside the
camp" until they were proven well (Lev. 13:45–46). Both men and
women with certain bodily discharge were "put out of the camp"
until the discharge ceased, along with those who had touched the
dead (Num. 5:2 ESV).

In a world where some of us grew up ashamed to pass tampons
to our friends when others might be watching, it can be difficult
to imagine the public humiliation of everyone in our community
knowing when we're on our period, having weird discharge, or
struggling with a rash of unknown origin. When we compound
that awkwardness with the fact that these folks also had to be banished from community—cut off from making the sacrifices that
brought them close to God—it's hard to imagine worse shame.

The message Moses is giving the people of Israel may not be
readily apparent to us, but he is letting them know that we serve a

God who is holy. Set apart. Without fault or blemish. And Moses is also setting up the scene of just how far that very same God is willing to go in order to bring the faulty and blemished back into his forever-presence.

The Insiders on the Outside

This is the stage that was set when the woman with the issue of blood grasped onto the hem of Jesus's garment (Mark 5:25–34). This is the context from which Jesus healed the lepers (Luke 17:12–19).

Here comes this man who is unafraid of those whom the Israelites would have labeled unclean, unworthy, shameful—who were not fit to stand in the presence of a holy God. Here comes a man who *is* that holy God wrapped in flesh, who draws near to the sick and ashamed, who offers them healing and acknowledgment in a culture that had grown to disdain them.

What was Jesus doing in all of these healing events? What was the point? On a literal and temporary level, he was healing them of that which caused them to be cast out, so they could be brought back into communal fellowship with their people. And on a spiritual level, he was pointing to what he had come to do permanently by means of the cross. Through his suffering on the cross, he was going to bring back those who were cast off from God's presence.

See how Hebrews 13:11–14 explains this:

> For the bodies of those animals whose blood is brought into the most holy place by the high priest as a sin offering are burned outside the camp. Therefore, Jesus also suffered outside the gate, so that he might sanctify the people by his

own blood. Let us, then, go to him outside the
camp, bearing his disgrace. For we do not have
an enduring city here; instead, we seek the one
to come.

As we can see, the Old Testament sacrificial system has set us
up to understand the way Jesus's sacrifice would work. The bodies
of sacrificial animals were disposed of somewhere specific—outside
the camp, or, in other words, the place of unbelonging and shame.
Working as a substitute, the animal's body was cast off in the place
the people deserved to be for their sins. It took their place. Now
that their sin was atoned for by means of the body and blood of the
animal, and the animal went outside, the people could now sym-
bolically come back "inside"—into good standing with God. They
deserved to be on the outs with God, in other words. But because
of the sacrifice of the animal, they get to be welcomed back in.

And likewise, Jesus suffered, the writer of Hebrews says. As it
was with the animals, so it was with the sacrificial Savior. He suffered *outside* the city gate. He suffered in the place of humiliation,
in the location of shame. The in-crowd pushed him out, and he
bore not just the guilt, but the shame associated with such a scene.
All so *you* could be welcomed *in* God's presence.

This is so much better than relying on an animal sacrifice, for
animals have to be sacrificed over and over again. But Jesus's sacrifice was a *one*-time event, for *all* sin, never needing further sacrifices. *His* sacrifice works to the uttermost. When you cast your lot
with Jesus, *there is no more going in and out of the Father's welcome
and embrace.* You are always in, because the payment for the sin has
been fully paid, the shame fully borne. *The Father's gate is always
open to you,* beloved.

Notice the logic of how the passage ends: "Let us, then, go to him outside the camp, bearing his disgrace. For we do not have an enduring city here; instead, we seek the one to come" (vv. 13–14).

When we hitch our wagon to Christ, we can expect to be pushed outside of the same sort of camps that he was. In some way, we'll be an outsider. But we don't care about losing face before temporary, earthly communities that force members in and out on a whim each day. They can cast us out all they want. Because we belong to an enduring, eternal community—one that will last forever in a heavenly city. Remember, every gospel comes with its own people group, and the people group of Jesus's gospel is the church. This is what the writer of Hebrews means when he says "we have no lasting city" here on earth; rather, "we seek the city that is to come" (v. 14 ESV). More on this in the concluding chapter, but for now, know this: in that city, the gates are always open to you.

Friend, you may be cast out of the world's communities at various points in your life, forced into the place of shame from an earthly perspective. But as you are shoved outside of some "camp," you're actually not alone, for Christ is there. And with him, alongside all other believers in him that make up the global church, you belong. You bear reproach and scorn just like he did, yes, but you do not lack a place to call home, a place to be welcomed. For outside the camp of this world is where he dwells, and as a Christian, it's your residence too.

This is the irony that Hebrews is getting at. Sure, you may be cast out into the place of shame from a worldly perspective when you unite yourself to Christ. You may have to feel the pain of being an outsider. But in the eyes of heaven, and for eternity, you are actually more welcomed, secure, and provided for than the world can dream of being. When it comes to where you stand with God and his people, you're an insider. Your guilt has been paid for and your shame has been fully removed—which means you are forever welcomed in the courts of our God and *you can never be thrown out.*

Where all false gospels fail, the gospel of Jesus Christ prevails. Your shame is indeed removed. And your place of belonging, permanent.

Consider how Eugene Peterson's translation puts it:

> In the old system, the animals are killed and the bodies disposed of outside the camp. The blood is then brought inside to the altar as a sacrifice for sin. It's the same with Jesus. He was crucified outside the city gates—*that* is where he poured out the sacrificial blood that was brought to God's altar to cleanse his people.
>
> So let's go outside, where Jesus is, where the action is—not trying to be privileged insiders, but taking our share in the abuse of Jesus. This "insider world" is not our home. We have our eyes peeled for the City about to come. Let's take our place outside with Jesus, no longer pouring out the sacrificial blood of animals but pouring out sacrificial praises from our lips to God in Jesus' name. (Heb. 13:11–15 MSG)

This right here is what the healing of the lepers was all about, friend. As Jesus healed all those castaways in the Gospels, restoring them to the communities that they once stood at a distance from,

Jesus was giving object lesson after object lesson to make clear what he had come to do on a much larger scale—bringing those who were banished outside of God's city gates (which is all of us) back into right relationship, fellowship, and belonging. *Forever.*

Never Cast Out

Now that we know these details about "the place outside the camp" in Old Testament times, and the purpose of Jesus's mission as he ministers to the types of people who sit outside the city gates, the language of "casting out" in John 6:37–40 (ESV) takes on new meaning:

> "All that the Father gives me will come to me, and whoever comes to me I will never cast out. For I have come down from heaven, not to do my own will but the will of him who sent me. And this is the will of him who sent me, that I should lose nothing of all that he has given me, but raise it up on the last day. For this is the will of my Father, that everyone who looks on the Son and believes in him should have eternal life, and I will raise him up on the last day."

I'm going to say it again: he will *never* cast us out. No matter what. The old law has been fulfilled in the person and work of Jesus Christ. There are none too sick to draw near to him, none too feeble to stand in his presence. There is no shame too great for him to cover with his matchless love. If you have come to him, believing in his substitutionary work on your behalf, *you cannot be plucked from his hand.* Hear his words to you:

"My sheep hear my voice, I know them, and they follow me. I give them eternal life, and they will never perish. **No one will snatch them out of my hand.** My Father, who has given them to me, is greater than all. No one is able to snatch them **out of the Father's hand**." (John 10:27–29)

Beloved, we have been sealed for all eternity. God hasn't made a covenant with us by degrees. We are his. All in—100 percent. Nothing can separate us from him, and no aspect of his love for us is pending any outside approval. It's done. It's finished.

This is the better message. *This* is the gospel that prevails over all other gospels. This is the only way to remove shame, and it's the only way to get the forever, permanent, never-wears-out sort of belonging your heart aches for. So when you find yourself trying to throw shame off some other way, for all that's good, remember this gospel.

Remember this Christ.

Remember the people you belong to and the true gates you sit inside of.

Remember the truth when false messages start swirling around you, and say: "*I already have good news about my shame* being removed, so I don't need this other gospel, and on top of that, *I already belong*."

Here and Now

Okay, you might be thinking. *I'm tracking. And I'm loving this gospel freedom from shame. But what about the fact that people who are saved still sin? Shouldn't they be ashamed about that? And what about when I sin and feel subsequent shame? I mean, if Christ already removed my shame, what do I do on the days it comes rolling back in?*

Good questions, as these get at the tension we talked about back in chapter 4: the "already-and-not-yet" point on the time line of redemption, where we sit in between Christ's first and second coming. Meaning, there are realities about our experience with God that are already true in Christ, and yet not experienced in full on this side of the resurrection. The *power* of shame has been fully defeated, but not the *presence* of shame. Its ghost still haunts us. Which means we must remind ourselves that though the death of shame is already complete, we must, as we do with sin, war against it daily. We must remember that the death of shame on the cross will echo in myriad "little deaths" as we go about this Christian life. Said more succinctly, we will constantly have to put shame to death as we put our sin to death (Rom. 8:12–13).

The good news in this hard work is that even as these things war in our lives, we are no longer *defined* by them. We are no longer defined by our sin because Christ has redeemed us. We are no longer motivated by our shame, because, through Christ's perfect sacrifice, our shame has been covered. Indeed, because we are no longer slaves to sin or to shame, we can now walk in obedience not out of fear of being cast out, but out of *love* for all our Savior has done for us. We walk like Christ *because* we belong to him, not because we're *trying* to belong to him. And in doing so, we walk the Christian life out totally free of shame as our motivator.

How? you may wonder. *If the presence of shame still lingers here and now in this "in-between" stretch of time, still tempting me at every turn to be motivated by it or held captive to it, doesn't that mean I'll need some powerful tools to help fight it off?*

Great question.

And as it turns out, part 3 holds exactly the tools you're looking for.

Living in the Middle

CHAPTER 7

Silencing the Accuser

M y third son was born six weeks before my last book came out.

If you have never written a book, you might not know writing the book is only half of the work—the other half starts just before the book comes out. Countless interviews, reviews, launch events, and social media posts were coming down the pike, and I wasn't sure if I could handle them all. So I asked my publisher if we could push the more formal parts of the marketing process out by a few months, while still promising to make a splash about the book on my social feeds.

My publisher very graciously agreed to this, but, of course, I still felt pressure to make my soft launch a success. And to do that, I knew it required connecting directly to readers in order to get the word out and, hopefully, drum up some interest. To that end, I spent hours on social media promoting my book through educational posts, Q&As, and links.

During all of this, my newborn was . . . newborning.

One day I posted apologizing for the delay on some promised content, explaining that my baby had kept me up all night. I posted one of his nighttime feeding schedules with my readers: he was up at 12:38 a.m., 1:50 a.m., 3:23 a.m., 5:38 a.m., and 7:40 a.m. (I knew this because I was drowning under the weight of intense postpartum anxiety, and was logging every feeding session, diaper change, and wake—an endeavor that was probably helpful in theory, but just fed my neurosis in practice). In a weak jab at humor (and now I see, in efforts to avoid shame), I quipped:

> *I know someone will respond to me by saying, "That's what he's supposed to do!" Third child. I'm aware. But I'm also exhausted because I'm more than just a milk receptacle. At least . . . I think I am? Hard to say these days.*

Of the responses I received, 99.9 percent were from fellow mothers of newborns, moms who remembered those days, or women who had never experienced those days but empathized with the thought of losing that much sleep.

But of course, there's always that one. Here's what it said:

> Does this imply that those of us who do nurse on demand and fully commit ourselves to these super tough newborn days with babies are "just a milk receptacle?" If babies need to do these things to thrive and we mothers sacrifice nearly everything to allow our babies to thrive, then it seems to me we are doing the best work God has given us to do IN THIS SEASON. Not for all time, not reducing us to mere animals like cows, but we are literally the sole

> living human who is sustaining the life of another whole human, just like pregnancy. Even though I have felt this sense of "I'm just a milk machine and have no life," why is that wrong/bad? It is only for a very short season in life, and that work is incredibly valuable, right? It does seem to me like you (in the same ways I have) struggle with this season of new motherhood to a newborn, even it if it is your third. In this culture, we think sleep and work outside of the home are our rights. But are they with a newborn?

By the time I received that message, I knew that I was writing a book about shame.

We've mentioned before how asking God to teach us about shame can feel like inviting shame to sit down across from you and have it out with you once and for all.

This was my moment.

When I got that message, I briefly considered that I shouldn't have asked God to teach me about shame, because doing so seemed to open the floodgates for shame to come roaring into my life, beckoning me down the rabbit hole of manifold shame-spirals every single day.

Silencing the Accuser

In the book of Revelation, the apostle John paints a vivid picture of Satan as our accuser:

> Now war arose in heaven, Michael and his angels
> fighting against the dragon. And the dragon and

his angels fought back, but he was defeated, and there was no longer any place for them in heaven. And the great dragon was thrown down, that ancient serpent, who is called the devil and Satan, the deceiver of the whole world—he was thrown down to the earth, and his angels were thrown down with him. And I heard a loud voice in heaven, saying, "Now the salvation and the power and the kingdom of our God and the authority of his Christ have come, for the accuser of our brothers has been thrown down, who accuses them day and night before our God. And they have conquered him by the blood of the Lamb and by the word of their testimony, for they loved not their lives even unto death. Therefore, rejoice, O heavens and you who dwell in them! But woe to you, O earth and sea, for the devil has come down to you in great wrath, because he knows that his time is short!" (12:7–12 ESV)

Who is the "ancient serpent" John talks about in verse 9?
He's none other than the serpent who showed up in Genesis 3.
And what is this serpent doing in Revelation 12:10?
He's doing the same thing he did in Genesis 3:5.
He's hurling accusations.
Before we dive into the picture in Revelation, recall what the serpent said to Eve when he first approached her in the garden. After planting a seed of doubt with the words, "Did God really say?" (Gen. 3:1), he outright accuses God of lying (Gen. 3:5). The serpent posits that God, who has given every good gift to his

children in the garden, is now holding out on them. The fruit won't *kill* them, the serpent argues—it will make them more like God. In essence, he is *accusing* the God of the universe of falsehood.

We have already talked about the rest of the story. The birth of shame follows quickly after this first accusation and the resulting disobedience to God. But God doesn't leave Adam and Eve in the hands of the accuser. He promises in verse 15 that the accuser will someday be silenced, once and for all, by the "seed" of the woman (KJV).

We now know that the silencer of the accuser is Jesus Christ.

So, you may wonder, *if God promised to silence the accuser in Genesis—and Jesus came onto the scene in Matthew—then why are we still dealing with the accuser in Revelation?*

Well, remember the "already-and-not-yet" situation we discussed in the last chapter? It applies here. Satan was ultimately defeated the moment God said he would be because God's Word is bond. Christ's death obliterated any chance for Satan to have dominion over God's children.

And yet, Satan is still roaming the earth like a roaring lion, seeking who he can devour (1 Pet. 5:8). His ultimate power over us has been taken away, but not his presence on this earth. For now, he is still accusing the brethren *day and night before our God* (Rev. 12:10). It is not until the end of days in this apocalyptic book of the Bible that Satan is finally silenced *for good.*

He has already lost the war, but he is grappling for victory in every little skirmish. He has already been defeated, but he wants to take as many faithful moments of the brethren down with him as he possibly can. "He knows his time is short" (Rev. 12:12), and he is ramping up his battle cry against the anointed in a desperate attempt to go down with a fight.

The Pilgrim's Progress is the allegorical journey of a Christian walking through his life of faith. He is bound for the Celestial City—an eternity spent with Christ. Along the way, he is beleaguered by so many of the things that we face in our own Christian walk: doubt, fear, and shame.

When Christian comes upon Apollyon—John Bunyan's representation of the devil—this iteration of the serpent opens his mouth to do what he does best: he is here to accuse the brethren. Reminding Christian of every faltering step he has taken along his faith journey, Apollyon says:

> "Thou didst faint at first setting out, when thou wast almost choked in the gulf of Despond. Thou didst attempt wrong ways to be rid of thy burden, whereas thou shouldst have stayed till thy Prince had taken it off. Thou didst sinfully sleep, and lose thy choice things. Thou wast almost persuaded also to go back at the sight of the lions. And when thou talkest of thy journey, and of what thou hast seen and heard, thou art inwardly desirous of vainglory in all that thou sayest or doest."[7]

How many times have we heard similar barbs from the accuser? Didn't we almost slip into despondency that one time we were called to trust God? Didn't we try to shake off our burdens in our own strength, without trusting the goodness of our wise Father in heaven? Weren't we asleep when we should have been alert to the voice of God? Didn't we halt in the face of difficulty and consider that we had perhaps made the wrong choice in following Jesus? And when we did well, didn't we struggle with vanity?

The voice of shame doesn't always speak to us in outright lies. Sometimes, it accuses us with selective bits of truth. We *are* weak. We *do* falter. We *have* sinned.

I have told you all of the ways that Christian could have answered Apollyon.

He could have said, "Listen, man, no one's perfect. It's our imperfections that make us so special. I'm beautiful just the way I am and I will not have you casting doubt on my journey."

He could have said, "I know. You're right. I'm just going to use these accusations to try to do better and prove you wrong. The next time you speak to me, you won't have *anything* to say, because I'm going to perfect myself!"

He could have said, "Look, I know I did all of those things, but have you seen that guy over there? He's doing them *way* worse than I am."

And of course, finally, he could have said, "You're right. I'll never deserve to be on this journey. I'm going to pick up my pack and go back home."

Even if you haven't read *The Pilgrim's Progress*, I bet you can guess that Christian didn't give any of these responses. Instead, he said:

> "All this is true, and much more which thou hast left out; but the Prince whom I serve and honor is merciful, and ready to forgive. But besides, these infirmities possessed me in thy country, for there I sucked them in, and I have groaned under them, been sorry for them, and have obtained pardon of my Prince."[8]

Christian's words are the clarion call of the book you hold in your hands. The way to escape from shame is not to deny our imperfections. It's not to embrace our imperfections while ignoring the righteousness we have been called to. It's not to try harder. It's not to just *be* better.

No, Christian. The antidote to shame is right there in Genesis 3: it's the seed of the woman who will crush the head of the serpent; it's the sacrifice that clothes us more thoroughly than fig leaves ever could.

It's right there in Revelation 12: it's the blood of the Lamb, the sacrifice foretold in Genesis 3 and delivered on the cross.

It's right there in Christian's words—it's the pardon of our Prince. It's the pardon he obtained on the cross by dying in our stead and taking on shame once and for all.

Christian's words had the effect of a bucket of water on the Wicked Witch of the West: Apollyon had a complete and utter meltdown. Bunyan tells us he "broke out into a grievous rage." He changed tactics, attacking Christian outright.

Spoiler alert: he was not victorious.

Because Satan never can be over God's elect.

Christian's praise at the end of this encounter echoes Revelation 12:

> "Great Beelzebub, the captain of this fiend,
> Designed my ruin; therefore to this end
> He sent him harness'd out; and he, with rage
> That hellish was, did fiercely me engage:
> But blessed Michael helped me, and I,
> By dint of sword, did quickly make him fly:

Therefore to Him let me give lasting praise,
And thank and bless his holy name always."[9]

Friend, *that's* your power as you live in between the beginning of shame's story and its final end. When shame comes knocking at your door, you can silence hell's accuser the same way Christian did. *You're right, Satan. I'm probably terrible at all the things you're telling me I'm terrible at. I've probably failed in all the ways you've accused me of, and more. And yet, miracle of miracles, I handed each failure to Jesus, and he has paid for each and every one. I once groaned under the weight and torment of such sins, but when I repented and came to the Savior, he bore the burden for me and now I am free. The weight is lifted off. I am pardoned forevermore in God's courtroom, which means you have no claim here. Wherever your accusations are true, they are already paid for. Either take it up with the Prince who pardoned me or go back to where you came from.*

Don't Let the Devil Use You

Accusations don't always come to us straight from the mouth of a talking serpent.

If they did, they'd probably be a lot easier to field.

They don't even always come to us from the devil himself, or even people who are actively in league with the devil.

Sometimes, they come from people who are incredibly well-intentioned—like I believe the mother in my first story to have been.

She saw a young mother delirious with exhaustion, trying to figure out how to balance work and a newborn and her identity and her sanity. And to bolster that young mama up with some good old-fashioned bootstrap theology . . . she shamed her.

She shamed this mother . . . for needing sleep.

In the South, we have a saying: "Don't let the devil use you."

After my first baby, this message would have been an example of the *perfect* instrument that the devil could use to broker an Apollyon-esque showdown in my heart. I would have read each sentence and felt the heavy burden of shame dripping in every phrase. Children are a *gift.* You should be *grateful.* You *chose* to be a mother. Your body is not yours anymore. Your highest calling, at least right now, is to mother that baby. Any time you feel the least bit exhausted or discouraged, it's because you've made an idol.

Don't let your voice echo the voice of the accuser, Christian. Let your voice be seasoned with the balm of the gospel.

Let's pause here and look again at the pointed message I received, examining the accusations therein, one by one, and then let's see how a Scripture-soaked, gospel-centered approach can help us process such a message. (And before we begin, let me remind you of something I already mentioned in the introduction of this book, because it bears repeating. I realize that using such an example in a book on shame might feel trivial compared to deeper and darker ways shame manifests itself in our lives. And I'm using something trivial on purpose for two reasons; 1) I'm not a counselor or a trauma specialist, and 2) because it's the little, seemingly insignificant instances of shame that we almost always neglect. And the longer we don't pay attention to them, the more they pile up, and the more they pile up, the more we walk through our *entire* day totally blind to the fact that shame was both our motivator and interpreter.)

So here we go. Let's work through an example of what it could look like to handle accusations in light of Christ's gospel and God's Word.

> **Does this imply that those of us who do nurse on demand and fully commit ourselves to these super tough newborn days with babies are "just a milk receptacle"?**

"Those of us who nurse on demand" and "those of us who fully commit ourselves."

The accusation: you are not fully committed to your newborn, or you wouldn't be saying how tired you are.

The truth: we are but flesh, and we do get exhausted. How amazing is it, then, that we have a Caretaker who doesn't have need for sleep, and is fully present for us whenever we need him (Ps. 121:1)?

> **If babies need to do these things to thrive and we mothers sacrifice nearly everything to allow our babies to thrive, then it seems to me we are doing the best work God has given us to do IN THIS SEASON.**

The accusation: you are not putting your baby first and you are not showing a willingness to sacrifice your body for the good of your child.

The truth: we are indeed called to be living sacrifices . . . for God (Rom. 12:1). We are called to make that sacrifice, not alone, but in community as the body of Christ, serving together (Rom. 12:4–5).

Not for all time, not reducing us to mere animals like cows, but we are literally the sole living human who is sustaining the life of another whole human, just like pregnancy. Even though I have felt this sense of "I'm just a milk machine and have no life," why is that wrong/bad?

The accusation: you are solely responsible for sustaining your child, and that should be enough of an identity for you, at least in this season.

The truth: our identity is hidden in Christ in every season (Gal. 3:27–28). The work that we do *never* defines us the way that the work that Jesus has done on our behalf defines us.

It is only for a very short season in life, and that work is incredibly valuable, right? It does seem to me like you (in the same ways I have) struggle with this season of new motherhood to a newborn, even it if it is your third. In this culture, we think sleep and work outside of the home are our rights. But are they with a newborn?

The accusation: you are falling for the lies of the culture by believing that you are entitled to sleep or entitled to the creative outlet of your job. Really, you are entitled to neither.

The truth: humans, made creaturely by Christ himself at the dawn of time, were made by him in such a way as to need sleep in order to survive. That was his design, not ours. And it is a good design. Humans, as they image the God who is Creator, create all the time without trying—formal creative outlet or not. Indeed, there are seasons we do this in different ways and at different levels of capacity, but there's no turning it off because it's built into the human condition.

Can you imagine if we responded to the psalmist like this?

My enemies surround me.

David, you chose to be a warrior. Your enemies are going to surround you sometimes.

My tears have been my food, day and night.

David, you are a literal king. You have actual food you can eat. Stop being dramatic.

You have forgotten me.

David, God never forgets anything. Repent of your feelings.

If I sound foolish, I should. We know full well that when David came before God with his feelings—his anger, his sadness, his depression, his joy, his sorrow—God was fully capable of hearing and answering every single prayer.

He *knows* we are mere dust, beloved (Ps. 103:14).

Not only does he know it in the sense that he knows everything as the Lord of the universe—he knows it because he entered our reality by being born a baby and going through life experiencing the fragility of our humanity (Heb. 4:15).

We serve a Savior who literally wept tears of *blood* as he considered the weight of obedience to the Father (John 11:35). He didn't weep because he was sinful—Jesus knew no sin (2 Cor. 5:21). He wept because he was *human.*

Sometimes, the accuser uses our sin to fuel his accusations. Sometimes, though, he just uses our *humanness.*

Put another way, sometimes, Satan accuses us of the bad things we have done. But sometimes, he accuses us just for needing God in the first place.

Saying "I'm tired" isn't any more of a sin than saying, "I'm hungry" or "I'm thirsty." But wielded in the hands of the accuser, it becomes difficult to know the difference between sin we need to repent of, and shame that's just there to take our eyes off the cross.

The good news? Whether shame comes directly from the devil or someone being used by him—whether it comes from bad things we have done, or is just a result of our humanity—whether it comes from someone ill-intentioned or someone well-intentioned—whether we are in a place to discern all of those facts or not . . . the response is always the same.

We run to Jesus, and we trust in the gospel work he's done on our behalf—a work that gives us not only a better covering to hide behind, a better image to be conformed into, and a better message to believe, but a stronger Victor to shut the mouth of Satan.

I Believe—Help My Unbelief

So many of us believe that Jesus loves us and that he died for us. Some of us have heard that truth our entire lives. But we often fail to see how that truth ministers to us *right now.*

> What then shall we say to these things? If God is for us, who can be against us? He who did not spare his own Son but gave him up for us all, how will he not also with him graciously give us all things? Who shall bring any charge against God's elect? It is God who justifies. Who is to condemn?

Christ Jesus is the One who died—more than
that, who was raised—who is at the right hand of
God, who indeed is interceding for us. Who shall
separate us from the love of Christ? Shall tribu-
lation, or distress, or persecution, or famine, or
nakedness, or danger, or sword? As it is written,

"For your sake we are being killed all the day
long; we are regarded as sheep to be slaughtered."

No, in all these things we are more than conquerors through him who loved us. For I am sure
that neither death nor life, nor angels nor rulers,
nor things present nor things to come, nor pow-
ers, nor height nor depth, nor anything else in all
creation, will be able to separate us from the love of
God in Christ Jesus our Lord. (Rom. 8:31–39 ESV)

In Romans 8, Paul has made a case for what life looks like for
those who are in Christ Jesus—and he begins with the truth that
there is *no* condemnation for us. We will return to the first part of
chapter 8 in our next chapter, but I want to look at the closing: *If
God is for us, who can be against us?*

Read those words again. If God did not spare his own Son
from death on a cross, what makes us think that there is *anything*
the accuser can say that will shake his love for us? Who can bring a
charge against God's elect—the people who, Paul tells us earlier in
the passage, have been called, justified, and will be glorified according to his purposes? Who can condemn us when *the very judge* has
declared us pure?

What can separate us from the love of Christ?

Nothing, friend. Absolutely nothing. In fact, we are already more than conquerors in Christ. The "already" part in the "already-and-not-yet" tells us how the story ends. We *cannot* be separated from Jesus by the threats of the accuser.

Understanding that Jesus is our current Intercessor and Advocate *right now* in heaven at the right hand of the Father (as discussed in chapter 4) gives us the confidence to silence the accuser's voice. We have a representative in the courtroom of heaven who always wins when defending us.

He will always win.

Run Away from Yourself

We run to Jesus even if it means running *away* from ourselves.

The reason why the message at the beginning of this chapter had the potential to be so damaging for me is because I could have written it myself, once upon a time—*to* myself.

Sometimes, the devil accuses us.

Sometimes, well-meaning people echo Satan's accusations.

Sometimes, though? The best weapon in the accuser's arsenal is our own self-talk.

We can be our own worst enemies in this battle against shame. The way we talk to ourselves matters. The way we motivate ourselves matters. What we choose to focus on in our quest toward the Celestial City matters.

Speaking for myself, I have often echoed the shameful messages that I imbibed as a young woman. My husband would come home after I'd been with the kids all day and I would immediately launch into a litany of apologies that the house wasn't clean, that dinner wasn't quite ready, or that I wanted to take a nap and wasn't up to spending time together.

I will never forget my new husband throwing me a quizzical look and saying, "Jasmine. You don't work for me. We're both adults. I trust that you worked hard today."

Now, here's where my naysayers might be struggling: What if I *didn't* work hard? What if I *had* been lazy at home all day? Shouldn't that shame spur me to work harder?

It could. But I believe there's a better way forward.

We'll discuss it in the next chapter.

CHAPTER 8

The Power of Godly Compassion, Good Grief, God's Spirit, and God's Word

Remember that story I told about my first boyfriend's mother sending me that intense email?

To recap: she had been a mentor of mine before I started dating her son. My relationship with her began to unravel during the dating period. And afterwards, we exchanged a few words that are still emblazoned on my mind a decade later. The death knell in that email was: "It would appear that you were crushed under the weight of your own doubt and fears. Don't blame me for that."

Years later, that relationship came up in therapy, and I realized something: even though I had been humiliated by my first brush with heartache, the boy who hurt me wasn't the pain I most remembered. The sharpest sting came from his mother.

In the years since the incident, I've been able to understand why. Because I had trusted her with the deep well of insecurities I had, she had the very tools she needed to wound me. She shot a fiery arrow at me and her aim was sure. I thought about that email for days.

I thought about that email for months.

I thought about that email for years.

My doubts and fears are my constant companions. And one of the worst fears that I have causes me to doubt the love of people who uncover my flaws. In that email, my worst nightmare came true: I had been weighed and found wanting, and everyone knew it.

Get Thee Behind Me

One of the craftiest tools of the Enemy is his ability to use others as a mouthpiece. We talked about this a little bit in the last chapter: "Don't let the devil use you."

In Matthew 16, Jesus is explaining his imminent death to his disciples:

> From that time Jesus began to show his disciples that he must go to Jerusalem and suffer many things from the elders and chief priests and scribes, and be killed, and on the third day be raised. (v. 21 ESV)

Upon hearing Jesus talk about his suffering, his death, and his resurrection, good ol' Peter (who we can always trust to be the mouthy one), pulls Jesus to the side and rebukes him: "Far be it from you, Lord! This shall never happen to you" (v. 22 ESV).

Jesus replies with the lines that chill us:

"Get behind me, Satan! You are a hindrance to me.
For you are not setting your mind on the things of
God, but on the things of man." (v. 23 ESV)

Not, "Hey, Peter, your thinking is a little off here, my dude."
Not, "Well, that's one way to interpret things." Not even, "I don't
need you to distract me from what God is calling me to do right
now."

No. Jesus says, in the KJV flair: *"Get thee behind me, Satan."*

Now, we know that Peter is not actually Satan. In fact, by vir-
tue of his confession,[10] he goes on to become the rock on which
Jesus builds his very church. He clearly grows in his understanding of Christ's purpose on earth, the nature of salvation, and the
responsibility of his disciples. He extolls these things beautifully in
two New Testament epistles.

But if we fast-forward to the garden of Gethsemane, we see
the fully man nature of Jesus quaking at the coming reality of his
painful death on the cross. He is so anguished at his impending
sacrificial death on the cross that he asks his Father if there is any
other way that redemption can be accomplished for his chosen ones
(Luke 22:42). He is so overcome with the thought of what he's
about to face that he weeps tears of blood (v. 44).

Jesus has gathered his disciples around him in the days leading
up to the brutal death he must die on their behalf, and instead of
encouraging Jesus and offering support and full-hearted allegiance
to God's plan of redemption, Peter becomes a hinderance.

I don't pretend to understand the intricacies of what it is to be
fully God and fully man. I don't pretend to know more than what
the Scriptures tell us about Jesus's thoughts and feelings in the days
leading up to his death. But I do know that anguish that culminates

in bloody tears doesn't just appear out of thin air. And I also know what it's like to have someone put their finger right into the wound of our deepest fear.

You know who loves it when that happens?

Satan.

Not in a "the devil is behind every bush and lurking in every alley" kind of way—but in a "don't do the devil's work for him as an accuser of the brethren" kind of way.

We know how Satan has acted in Jesus's life before, tempting him to step outside of God's plan and exert supremacy in Satan's way, not in God's way (Matt. 4:8–9). As inadvertently as Peter might have been doing this, he was walking a well-worn pattern: "Surely you can't die, Jesus. Did God *really* say?"

Did God Really Say . . . ?

We are not the Creator of the universe made flesh, so I don't advise indiscriminately bestowing the name of "Satan" on anyone who happens to step on the minefield of our shame-triggers. Sometimes, like the woman in the last chapter who reached out to me about saying I was tired after a sleepless night with my baby, people really aren't trying to be evil. Like Peter, they're trying to help. They just don't realize they are thinking according to the world instead of the gospel.

Sometimes, they're even speaking out of their own shame and trauma.

You see, Satan's "*did God really say*" doesn't just apply to temptation to disobey the law of God. It can also apply to the temptation not to believe what God has clearly spoken about us as his beloved sons and daughters.

Did God *really* say that he has cast your sins as far as the east is from the west (Ps. 103:12)?

Did Jesus *really* carry every ounce of our guilt and shame on the cross (Heb. 12:2)?

Can we *really* be confident in God's love for us, no matter what (2 Cor. 3:4)?

You see, we might think that we'd never be like Peter, rebuking Jesus after he spoke the truth about his purpose here on this earth. But how many times have we questioned the plain truths put forth for us in the Scriptures in the exact same way?

How many times have we ourselves spoken that doubt into our own lives?

Forget yelling "Get thee behind me, Satan" to a random lady on the Internet—how many times do we need to be reminded not to tell lies to *ourselves*?

Answering Human Accusers with Compassion

In 2020, the beginning of the pandemic, I started listening to *The Sorcerer's Stone* audiobook. Within the month, I had devoured all seven books in the Harry Potter series (*Half-Blood Prince* is the best one. Fight me.), chosen a favorite character (Neville Longbottom 5Ever), and picked my Hogwarts house (Ravenclaw. There is no competition).

In the third book, Professor Remus Lupin teaches his students how to face their fears by unleashing a creature called a *boggart* in the classroom.

A boggart takes the form of whatever its adversary fears the most. In the *Harry Potter* films, one student sees a clown. Ron sees a spider. Neville sees Professor Snape.

As each student walks up to the boggart and faces their fear, the creature quickly changes shape for its next opponent. Some of its forms might be terrifying for everyone in the room; some of its forms might only scare the person it's trying to scare. Some of the students' fears might make sense to their class. Some of those fears might make no sense at all. But the boggart's skill is in isolating the worst fear of whichever student it's facing down at that moment.

I'm not comfortable saying *Get thee behind me, Satan* to many people.

But I do think that sometimes, folks are quite good at acting like a boggart.

Sometimes, they see a weakness and mercilessly exploit it. Other times, though, they stumble upon our weaknesses while they're really just voicing fears of their own.

Let's return to that message I received from an internet mom as discussed in the last chapter—the one about what sacrifices we should be willing to make for a newborn baby (to read the message, see pages 146–147).

When I received that message, there were two people who needed compassion.

In the last chapter, we talked about how one of those people was me. In Peter fashion, this woman was giving a flesh-and-blood voice to the doubts that plague so many new mothers early on in their journeys: "Do I love my baby enough?" "Am I doing enough for my baby?" "Am I a bad mom if I get tired?"

It's easy to throw some serious shade at the lady who rebuked a new mom for admitting that she was tired and felt more machine than person in her hazy newborn days.

It might be harder to take a closer look at that message and show compassion to the messenger. What lies was this woman believing, not just about me, but about herself? What lies was she believing about her purpose or identity? In what ways was shame leading her around, just like it tries to lead me? In what hard place was no one there to help her, or offer her a safe place to be *human* instead of superwoman? In what context did she learn that the only way to handle life is to buck up, be invincible, or "get over it already"? How many times had someone kicked her while she was down? To what comfort was she turning in her own motherly exhaustion? If we assume she talks to herself like this, is it a very kind way for her to relate to herself?

Granted, I wasn't in much of a position to send her back a message about how valuable and cherished she is (mother or not), and how deserving of sleep and nurturing she is just by the sheer nature of being made in God's image. In my present mental state, the kindest thing I could do was withdraw, take the space I needed to examine my own thoughts, and hold my tongue.

As I have turned that interaction over in my head while writing this book, I have returned repeatedly to the fact that oftentimes, the vilest accuser we face is shouting out accusations from our own heart. Because if I hadn't been entertaining inklings of doubt about my own worth as a mother, her words wouldn't have wounded me quite as much as they did. And if my admission of exhaustion hadn't triggered her own shame in some way, she would not have messaged me about what I appeared to be "implying."

There we were: two wounded people in the perfect position to wound one another. There we were: two hurting people interacting with each other in ways that could multiply our hurt exponentially.

We both needed compassion.

The same is true for you and your accusers in this life. Sometimes you *know* when the voice of accusation swirling around in your head is from the Enemy himself, and in that moment, by all means, tell him where to go. But many other times—arguably most of the time—shame will roll out of the mouth of another human who is probably just as disoriented by this fallen world as you are. Chances are, your accusers have simply latched onto one of the terrible methods this world offers them of dealing with life's hardships, and they are applying it to you because that's the only method they've ever known. So, beloved, when angry accusations come to your door, answer the fiery figure in front of you with compassion. You'd be surprised at how effective this tool is at putting out the shame-flames.

And that's just *one* of the many tools God gives us.

Good Grief

Back in my teaching days, I loved a good rubric. It was one document, usually a single page, that told my students exactly how I would be grading their projects, essays, recitations, etc. A rubric is a humanities teacher's version of an answer key. Because English can so often be subjective, a rubric allows a teacher to set clear expectations of their students, even in a creative assignment. I could just put whatever I was grading through the rubric, assign the amount of points the rubric gave to each section, and then tally up their grade.

It was beautiful.

Inevitably, when I have this conversation about shame, someone will say, "Okay. I get how the example you provided was shaming. But how do I know the difference between the shame I feel when I really am guilty for doing something wrong, and the shame I feel that isn't due to genuine guilt or conviction over sin? When an accusation comes my way, how can I tell the difference?"

It would be amazing if this part of the chapter was a beautiful rubric with a grid that taught you exactly how to grade every accusation. You could tally up all the points and know whether what you're experiencing is godly conviction, or worldly shame. What I'll offer you instead is the Word of God.

To do this, I often return to 2 Corinthians 7:8–13:

> For even if I grieved you with my letter, I don't regret it. And if I regretted it—since I saw that the letter grieved you, yet only for a while—I now rejoice, not because you were grieved, but because your grief led to repentance. For you were grieved as God willed, so that you didn't experience any loss from us. For godly grief produces a repentance that leads to salvation without regret, but worldly grief produces death. For consider how much diligence this very thing—this grieving as God wills—has produced in you: what a desire to clear yourselves, what indignation, what fear, what deep longing, what zeal, what justice! In every way you showed yourselves to be pure in this matter. So even though I wrote to you, it was not because of the one who did wrong, or because of the one

who was wronged, but in order that your devotion
to us might be made plain to you in the sight of
God. For this reason we have been comforted.

For some quick context, here's what's happening: Before the
book of 2 Corinthians was written, Paul had written a previous
letter to the church in the ancient city of Corinth. There were
some not-good things happening in that church—things that were
wrong, out of step with the gospel, and out-of-bounds for proper
Christian living. Paul wrote to them to handle these not-good
things in a gut-level-honest, direct way. It was a severe letter to say
the least.

As 2 Corinthians tells us, it was a hard letter for them to receive;
indeed, it caused a deep grief at first. It stung. And yet, on the other
side of that grief, some good things come about that Paul mentions
overtly: these Corinthians have taken responsibility for their sin
and sought to take strong measures to make things right. They are
eager to clear themselves. They are zealous to settle the situation
and they are more reverent toward God. In their genuine spiritual
sorrow that they sinned against God, and they have made amends.

Paul calls their experience "godly grief." In our day, we'd probably call it the Holy Spirit's *conviction*. How does he know it's godly
instead of worldly? Because of its result. It led to life and flourish-
ing. It turned from sin, toward God, and corrected the mistake.
This is what "salvation without regret" means. A life that leaves
sin and pursues God, and in the end, will experience the salvation promised in the Scriptures. And though Paul is sad that these
Corinthians felt the bad feelings associated by his letter, he's grateful it was the right kind of bad feeling. It was good grief.

In contrast, "worldly grief" produces a different result: death. What Paul means by this is that there's a type of bad feeling in this world that does not move toward God in order to reconcile with him and correct one's mistakes. Instead of repenting, worldly sorrow wallows, languishes, and moves away from God. Why? Because worldly sorrow is sad about different things than godly sorrow. It is sad about losing the world's approval, sad that it did not meet some cultural expectation, or perhaps sad it got caught in sin. None of this is godly grief, for godly grief produces repentance and restoration. Worldly grief produces an endless cycle of self-flagellation.

In short, godly grief leads to reconnection with the God whom we have sinned against. Worldly grief leads to constant isolation because we will never, in and of ourselves, be good enough to connect with God.

There are some ways that we can tell the difference: Does the bad feeling we are experiencing point to guilt over a specific sin that we have committed against God, therefore grieving him? Can we see that sin clearly outlined in Scripture? Does the acknowledgment of that sin have a clear-cut road to repentance and restoration? Do we *want* restoration with God? Is the result of the bad feelings moving you *toward* God and correcting the mistake?

It might be godly grief.

Is the charge nebulous? Is it something that we can't repent of because it's not exactly sin? Does acknowledging it move us toward repentance and restoration, or does it keep us in a constant holding pattern of never being good enough to accept the salvation that God has freely offered us in Jesus? What is truly causing our sadness—crossing a line with God and therefore grieving him, or crossing a cultural line with the world and losing its approval? Is the result of the bad feeling leading us *away* from God?

It might be worldly grief.

How, though? As powerful as godly grief is to help us fight shame in the "in between" times, how will you know the difference between it and worldly grief? Is there a rubric? How can you discern?

Through two more sources of power.

The Original Comforter

In John 14, Christ tells his disciples that even when he leaves them, they won't be alone.

> "These things I have spoken to you while I am still with you. But the Helper, the Holy Spirit, whom the Father will send in my name, he will teach you all things and bring to your remembrance all that I have said to you. Peace I leave with you; my peace I give to you. Not as the world gives do I give to you. Let not your hearts be troubled, neither let them be afraid. You heard me say to you, 'I am going away, and I will come to you.' If you loved me, you would have rejoiced, because I am going to the Father, for the Father is greater than I. And now I have told you before it takes place, so that when it does take place you may believe. I will no longer talk much with you, for the ruler of this world is coming. He has no claim on me, but I do as the Father has commanded me, so that the

world may know that I love the Father. Rise, let us
go from here." (vv. 25–31 ESV)

In this passage, we see a beautiful illustration of the Godhead. A full discussion of the Trinity is outside of the boundaries of this book, but the basics are that God the Father, God the Son, and God the Holy Spirit are all equally God. They are one God in three persons.

I know. The head-exploding emoji goes here.

God the Father sent God the Son to die on the cross for our sins. God the Son ascended into heaven, and God the Spirit dwells within us, teaching us and reminding us of all that Jesus taught us. We are sealed in the covenant with the Godhead by the Holy Spirit (Eph. 1:13), through whom we have access to the very mind of Christ (1 Cor. 2:16).

Let's look at one of my favorite passages in all of Scripture: 1 Corinthians 2.

> These things God has revealed to us through the Spirit. For the Spirit searches everything, even the depths of God. For who knows a person's thoughts except the spirit of that person, which is in him? So also no one comprehends the thoughts of God except the Spirit of God. Now we have received not the spirit of the world, but the Spirit who is from God, that we might understand the things freely given us by God. And we impart this in words not taught by human wisdom but taught by the Spirit, interpreting spiritual truths to those who are spiritual. (vv. 10–13 ESV)

You know how in 1 Corinthians 1:18–31, Paul says the gospel is foolishness to those who don't believe? He's returning to that point in 1 Corinthians 2. He's letting his listeners know that we understand the paradoxical truths of the gospel, not by our own power, not by our own knowledge, and not by our own wisdom, but by the power, knowledge, and wisdom of the Holy Spirit. It is only by the Spirit that we're able to interpret the spiritual.

In her book *Is the Bible Good for Women?*, Wendy Alsup talks about another area of our lives where we're tempted to beg for a rubric: biblical womanhood. In discussing how to properly apply Proverbs 31, she brings up the fact that the Proverbs aren't written as commands to live by (like the Ten Commandments), but, rather, as nuggets of wisdom that can be applied differently in different circumstances.

For example, Proverbs 26:4–5 might seem like it contradicts itself—but, it's giving us two pieces of wisdom that might be used differently in two different circumstances. Alsup writes:

> Wisdom is wise only when applied correctly in the right situation. A believer reading Proverbs 26, walking with the Holy Spirit, recognizes that there are times when engaging fools verbally will result in becoming like the fools she is trying to rebuke. She also recognizes that sometimes fools need someone to point out their foolishness so they won't believe their own hype. The Holy Spirit is our help in understanding the difference.[11]

How do we know when to apply Proverbs 26:4 or Proverbs 26:5? How do we know when our situation requires answering the fool according to his folly or letting that fool do his fool stuff on his own time? "The answer," Alsup tells us, "is to apply wisdom in ways that are actually wise through the indwelling Holy Spirit."[12]

Come back with me to 1 Corinthians 2:

> But the person without the Spirit does not receive what comes from God's Spirit, because it is foolishness to him; he is not able to understand it since it is evaluated spiritually. The spiritual person, however, can evaluate everything, and yet he himself cannot be evaluated by anyone. For "who has known the Lord's mind, that he may instruct him?" But we have the mind of Christ. (1 Cor. 2:14–16)

The Holy Spirit gives us access to the very *mind of Christ*.

I understand how this conversation can be frightening. How can we discern the calling of the Holy Spirit and the calling of our own flesh? How do we know if we're being true to what God commands or if we're just being true to what we want in the moment?

Alsup is helpful here again:

> You cannot read Proverbs the same way you read the Ten Commandments, yet many Christians fear situational wisdom. Some don't trust others to figure out what applies and how to apply it, so they enforce one-dimensional conclusions that don't allow for the nuances that much of the biblical proverbs offer. The answer to such fear is to apply wisdom in ways that are actually wise through the indwelling Holy Spirit. Paul exhorts

us to "walk by the Spirit" in Galatians 5:16 and to "keep in step with the Spirit" in 5:25. It is this pressing into God via the Spirit that equips you and me to apply wisdom in wise ways without fear of moral relativism. The Holy Spirit helps us distinguish principle from application and know what application God has for us, as opposed to what He has for some other person in a different situation.[13]

Alsup goes on to say that the main way the Spirit helps us to interpret God's will for us is through the Scriptures.

That's the rubric, folks.

Scripture Rubric

Because of the nature of this book, I have focused a lot on how the Spirit puts our worldly guilt to rest.

One of the jobs of the Holy Spirit is to testify to your spirit that you are, indeed, a child of God (Rom. 8:16). Even when you feel like you're not. Even when you forget. Even when shame is laid on thick. When you forget you are his child, and forever welcomed instead of cast out, you have his very Spirit within you to remind you.

I want you to remember that when you are ashamed, you do not have to run and hide like Adam and Eve in the garden. Instead, you can let the Spirit do his work. Don't quench the Spirit (1 Thess. 5:19). Let him testify the truth: that you are a child of the Most High God. That your salvation has been purchased by the blood of

Jesus. That *nothing* can separate you from the love of God (Rom. 8:38–39).

Let him testify to your spirit that you are a child of God, not a stranger or an enemy to him. Let him convince you to run back into the arms of the Father who wants to help you. If you've sinned, his help will look like giving you the power to change.

If you haven't sinned but are made to feel as if you have by someone you desperately you want approval from, his help will look like giving you the power to believe his approval is all that matters anyway.

In other words, if you're not actually in the wrong, He will help you start caring a lot less about the opinions of others who possibly think you are. Regardless of the reasons for why you're running, let the Spirit testify to the truth of what Christ has done. He's made you God's child. Enjoy that. Come out of hiding and run back to your Father. You don't have to hide anymore. You have a new covering. You have an image you're capable of being formed into. You have a better message to believe. Let the Spirit testify to these things.

And if you *have* sinned?

Friend, the same reminders apply.

As I've said before (and I hope it's sinking in now), because you have been bought with the blood of Christ, the antidote for godly guilt is the same as the antidote for worldly guilt: run to Jesus. Do the thing that Adam and Eve should have done in the garden and call out to the Father before he even comes looking for you. You are his beloved child—he will clothe you in the righteousness of his Son (Eph. 4:24) just like he clothed Adam and Eve when they became aware of their nakedness.

If you've sinned, don't run and hide from his voice. Proverbs 3:11–12 teaches us (and Heb. 12:6 reiterates) that the Lord reproves those whom he loves. And the Spirit powerfully testifies to the truth that the ultimate punishment for our sin has already been meted out on the cross. Lean into that power, into that truth, for doing so helps you turn down the volume on all the shame-shouting.

Four Tools to Fight Shame

Shame has a way of leaving us feeling exposed.

It's a theme we've returned to again and again in these pages.

It's why Adam and Eve sewed together fig leaves and hid from the Lord in the garden. And it's why we hide from the weight of shame as it crashes in on our own lives.

But just as God clothed Adam and Eve with a sacrifice, he has provided a way for us to be clothed in the face of shame's cruel exposing. With real, godly compassion, repentance, the work of the Holy Spirit, and the comfort of God's Word, God has got us covered. And even if that shame never disappears completely this side of heaven, we know that the closer we get to God, the more the whispers of eternity will drown out the shouts of shame.

In the next chapter, we'll talk about how Christian community dials up those whispers of eternity even louder—leaving that shame-noise puny by comparison.

CHAPTER 9

The Power of Healthy Community

The first time I went to therapy, I thought I was there to talk about my miscarriage.

I started dating my husband in March of 2014. We got engaged in June of 2014. We got married in October of 2014. I took a positive pregnancy test the week of Thanksgiving—in 2014. Shortly after Christmas, I had the ultrasound that told us that our first baby's little heart had stopped beating.

I remember sitting on the table as the tech nervously prodded my stomach, looking for my baby's heartbeat. Because I was under the care of a midwife, I got my scans at an ultrasound center—the techs were not allowed to make medical proclamations. So instead of being forthright with me and telling me that I was in the middle of a miscarriage, this poor woman just looked at me, pale and anxious in the wake of the silence on that black-and-white screen.

I waited until she left the room to burst into tears. And when she came back and knocked on the door, I dried my eyes, took a deep breath, and said with a sunny cheerfulness I did not feel: "Come in!"

My new husband was slack-jawed, both in the face of this new grief, and in the face of my Jekyll and Hyde impersonation. The entire time we were at the center, I was smiling reassuringly and telling everyone who cast their sad eyes on me that "these things happen" and "it's not your fault."

When we got to the car, I burst into chest-heaving sobs and told my husband, "*See?* I told you something was wrong. I told you it was too easy for us to get pregnant."

Fast-forward about eighteen months. I was well into my second trimester, and under the care of a new group of midwives. When my depression screening came back, they suggested I either consider medication or talking to someone. I went with the latter and told my brand-new counselor that I was there to talk to her about my anxiety about having another miscarriage.

She nodded, listening carefully, and writing things down. "So, you're the oldest of nine children," she said.

I nodded.

"And you're a pastor's kid. Your dad is pretty popular in certain circles."

I nodded again, a little confused about why we weren't getting down into the nitty-gritty of my constant feelings of doom surrounding my current pregnancy.

"There were . . . other Black families at your church?"

"One or two," I told her, and she wrote that down too.

"And you married your husband six months after you started dating him long-distance?"

Now, I was irritated, "Yes," I told her, my voice tight. Why was she focusing on things that had nothing to do with the reason I was here?

She took a deep breath, sensing my frustration, and put her pencil down. Leaning across the table, she angled her body toward me and said, "I want to talk to you about your baby, Jasmine. And I will. But there is a *lot* here. Have you ever talked to anyone about all of it?"

"I'm talking to you," I said.

"Have you ever talked to anyone *else* about it?" she pressed. "Like, friends? Your pastor? Your family?"

I didn't even think about the words before they flew out of my mouth in the same tenor they'd been said throughout my life: "Oh, that's family business. I don't talk about that."

We Don't Talk about . . .

At this writing, Lin-Manuel Miranda has struck gold again with the soundtrack for the Disney movie, *Encanto*. The song "We Don't Talk about Bruno" is everywhere. Long and worthwhile story short, the Madrigal family has a black sheep that they don't discuss, and his name is Bruno.

My household didn't have a black sheep, per se, but we had a *"we don't talk about . . ."* type of pact. My dad was a pastor, and as an unfortunate by-product of his ministry, we often felt like we lived in a glass house. As the oldest child, I felt the pressure to be the perfect poster child for homeschooling, courtship, and all things "biblical womanhood." I also felt the pressure—oftentimes unspoken and equally oppressive to my parents—to keep the hardship of living under a microscope to myself.

And to hide my depression, my frustration, and my loneliness from everyone who might want to use those things against my dad.

My name was once used in a campaign to get my dad to step down from his eldership.

One time, I sat in a meeting for two hours while another pastor's kid told me a litany of ways I had offended and upset them.

I dated another pastor's son, and when we broke up . . . well, we've already discussed what happened there.

In each instance, I swallowed my feelings for the good of others.

When that first elder apologized to me, I offered him instant forgiveness—because that's what I was "supposed" to do.

When those pastor's kids asked me if I had any grievances against them, I said no, and that I was so sorry for everything (both real and imagined) that I had done—because that's what I was "supposed" to do.

When my heart got broken, I pasted on a smile and told everyone that I was fine, and that courtships protect your heart from pain—because that's what I was "supposed" to do.

When I lost my first baby . . . what I was "supposed" to do was harder than it ever had been. And the veneer of perfection that I had painted on for everyone, even my own family, began to crack.

What my new counselor wanted to know was if there was anyone who knew who I was *behind* the mask I wore as the perfect daughter—the perfect parishioner—the perfect wife—the perfect mother.

And the answer was no. Not even my new husband—because we were still getting to know each other.

As you read these words, perhaps you can't relate to the life of a pastor's kid or a young adult trying to find her way in certain evangelical spaces. Maybe you don't know what it's like to be the only Black girl in the room. Maybe you haven't had difficult run-ins with pastors, and maybe you don't know what it's like to act out your first relationship in front of an entire church. Maybe you've always felt free to be honest with your parents, because you weren't afraid of burdening them, and didn't feel like you had to be strong for your younger siblings.

Maybe you do relate to some aspect of what I've shared.

Or maybe you've had other experiences where you had to put on a brave face. Maybe you walked through grief alone because you didn't want to be a burden to others. Maybe you hid your true feelings because you didn't think that your friends would be able to handle them. Maybe you wanted to portray a certain image to the world, at the expense of your own mental health and well-being.

Guess what often motivates that self-protection?

That's right: shame.

And guess what festers when we hide our weaknesses from others for fear that we won't be met with love and acceptance?

You got it, class: shame.

Exposure to Air

I got a gnarly third-degree burn while I was pregnant with my youngest. It was ghastly—the skin on the back of my hand looked like it belonged on a zombified cast member of *The Walking Dead*. I wanted to always keep a Band-Aid over it, but my doctor told me that it was best to let it air out as much as possible. "It will heal faster that way."

So, I exposed my ugly skin to the air. And every time someone who loved me saw it, they exclaimed, "Oh, Jasmine! What happened?"

And every time they asked, I would look down at my feet and tell them that my pregnancy brain was so chronic that I forgot that when you're cooking with pans on the stove, the handles of those pans get hot.

Nobody said, "Wow, Jasmine. You're such an idiot. You deserve that burn."

Nobody said, "I would never do something so stupid. Maybe looking at your ugly hand will remind you of how ugly and stupid you are until you die."

Nobody said, "That is really disgusting. I know you have to let it air out so it will heal, but I don't want to look at it."

You know what they said?

"I'm so sorry. That looks painful."

"That happened to me once. Goodness, I know it hurts."

"I have something at my house that might make it feel better. I'll drop it by this afternoon."

Every single one of my friends met my shame over the appearance of my hand and the reason for its appearance with love and acceptance. Of course, they did. They love me. And it's kind of a jerk move to make fun of your pregnant friend for a brand-new deformity.

Heart-hurts are a little bit like my gnarly burn. My MO is to try to hide them from the watching world because they're ugly, and I don't want other people to see them. I want them to heal in the darkness and not in the light. But instead of healing, they tend to fester and continue to eat away at me while they're under wraps.

And here's the thing: it is terrifying to open up about the shame that festers around those heart wounds. Because unlike the burn on the back of my hand, not every heart wound will be met with the understanding that my friends provided. Sometimes, people we love will disappoint us when we are vulnerable with them.

Sometimes, they *will* say (either outright or in other ways), "Wow, Jasmine. It seems like you brought that shame on yourself."

"I would never put myself in a position to experience that shame. I hope you learned a valuable lesson from it."

"That *is* really shameful. You probably should have kept it to yourself."

Safe, Yet Vulnerable

First Corinthians 13 has been quoted on many a Hallmark card and in many a wedding ceremony. The words have become so familiar that we might forget to mediate on their meaning. We might also see passages like 1 Corinthians 13 as one of those "easy" passages—Christianity 101. We feel like we get it already.

I assure you: we don't.

And I know we don't, because of the way that Paul sets up the passage in question:

> If I speak in the tongues of men and of angels, but have not love, I am a noisy gong or a clang-ing cymbal. And if I have prophetic powers, and understand all mysteries and all knowledge, and if I have all faith, so as to remove mountains, but have not love, I am nothing. If I give away all I

> have, and if I deliver up my body to be burned, but
> have not love, I gain nothing. (1 Cor. 13:1–3 ESV)

Paul lets us know that the things we might associate with tremendous and impressive faith—speaking in tongues, prophesying, understanding the complex, or being able to move mountains in faith—are *nothing* compared to whether or not we understand the call to love.

Paul then describes exactly what that love looks like:

> Love is patient and kind; love does not envy or
> boast; it is not arrogant or rude. It does not insist
> on its own way; it is not irritable or resentful;
> it does not rejoice at wrongdoing, but rejoices
> with the truth. Love bears all things, believes all
> things, hopes all things, endures all things. (1 Cor.
> 13:4–7 ESV)

This is the kind of love that we can trust with our deepest shame, friends.

This love patiently sits with us as we process those shameful moments, dividing the truth of conviction from the lies of Satan.

This love does not boast about what they would have done differently.

This love is not rude; it is tender with our wounds.

This love does not rush through our pain to get its own way, but sits with us for as long as it takes.

This love does not resent us for our weakness, but reminds us that God's love is made perfect in that weakness (2 Cor. 12:9).

This love does not rejoice in the wrongs that have been done to us; nor does it rejoice in recounting the wrongs that we have done.

This love rejoices in the truth of the fact that Jesus conquers our shame.

This love bears our burdens right alongside us (Gal. 6:2), this love hopes with us in the darkest moments (Rom. 12:15), and this love rides through the storms with us as Jesus does (Prov. 18:24).

This love allows us to be completely vulnerable about the shame that so often ravages our hearts in the darkness; this is the love that turns on the lights.

I know what you may be thinking: *Sounds nice, if you can get it—but where on earth do you get it?*

Maybe you've trusted someone with your shame, and they showed themselves to be untrustworthy, sharing it with others.

Maybe you've showed your hurt to someone and have been met with impatience and abandonment.

Maybe you've had someone who was supposed to have been a friend throw your shame back into your face.

Maybe you've had someone laugh at your pain and call you oversensitive.

Maybe you've had someone tell you to just get over it already.

Maybe you have someone resent you for your weakness or tell you that you deserve whatever shame has taken up residence in your heart.

I've been there, and it hurts. And our self-protecting impulses rise to the surface and tell us that trusting others is like putting our hands on a hot stove and just *asking* to get burned.

How do we override that alarm system that blares in our brains and tells us to *abort mission* whenever we think about trusting someone new?

Community of Faith

In the first half of Ephesians, Paul tells his listeners all about good doctrine. In the second half, he tells them how to apply that good doctrine to their lives.

Ephesians 4 begins:

> Therefore I, the prisoner in the Lord, urge you to walk worthy of the calling you have received, with all humility and gentleness, with patience, bearing with one another in love, making every effort to keep the unity of the Spirit through the bond of peace. There is one body and one Spirit—just as you were called to one hope at your calling—one Lord, one faith, one baptism, one God and Father of all, who is above all and through all and in all.
>
> Now grace was given to each one of us according to the measure of Christ's gift. (vv. 1–7)

As we see above, Paul admonishes us to *all humility and gentleness, with patience, bearing with one another in love, making every effort to keep the unity of the Spirit through the bond of peace*. This bond, he tells us, comes from the fact that we are all connected through the Holy Spirit—through one Lord, one faith, one baptism, and one God. And he tells us where the grace to walk in these fruits of the Spirit (Gal. 5:22–23) comes from . . . the bond that we have *in the Spirit*.

Yes, friends. This is like Sunday school, where every answer is "Jesus." Except the member of the Godhead who is constantly binding us together in unity with our brothers and sisters in Christ is the same one who helps us to determine whether we're feeling godly guilt or worldly guilt: the Holy Spirit.

The Godhead works together to bind hearts in the family of faith. God sent his Son to die on the cross so that we might live in perfect fellowship with Father, Son, and Holy Spirit. The Spirit dwells within us, connecting us to the very mind and heart of Christ. And the desire of that mind and heart is that we walk in love with our siblings in the faith, just as Christ walked in love toward us (Eph. 5:2).

I understand that sometimes, our visions for unity don't match up to our present reality, but it is so important to know God's intention for us. Because when others fall short, we need to understand that *people* are failing us; God's intentions for us are not what have failed. The search for people who understand and pursue this calling might be hard—it might be long—it might feel hopeless— but it is never in vain. Because as sure as there is a God in heaven, there are people existing on this earth who are walking about his purposes for them in community with others.

Do not try to bear your shame alone. A Christian community has the power to beat back shame in collective numbers; don't deprive yourself the chance to witness such a potent aid provided by the Lord. Whatever form it takes, no matter how many times a day its clouds come rolling in, *you need other people to help you weather it.*

Well, I should say you need *healthy* people to help you weather it.

Shame and Boundaries

In the last chapter, we talked about how, sometimes, people we love are inadvertently in the business of letting the devil use them.

When it comes to opening ourselves up to others and letting our shame see the light so it can heal, we need to make sure that we're being good stewards of our vulnerability. My burn needed air to heal, but if that air would've been toxic, whipping off my Band-Aid would have proved counterproductive.

Boundaries is such a scary term, I know. We often think of selfishness when we hear it: someone who walks around labeling anyone who gets on their nerves as toxic and writing them off at the slightest provocation. We might think of someone who doesn't know how to get along well with others and continues in unhealthy patterns under the guise of "healthy" boundaries that are anything but.

Whenever I talk about boundaries, I get some version of, "That's not very Philippians 2 of you." You might know the passage—Philippians 2:1–11 (esv):

> So if there is any encouragement in Christ, any comfort from love, any participation in the Spirit, any affection and sympathy, complete my joy by being of the same mind, having the same love, being in full accord and of one mind. Do nothing from selfish ambition or conceit, but in humility count others more significant than yourselves. Let each of you look not only to his own interests, but also to the interests of others. Have this mind among yourselves, which is yours in Christ Jesus,

who, though he was in the form of God, did not count equality with God a thing to be grasped, but emptied himself, by taking the form of a servant, being born in the likeness of men. And being found in human form, he humbled himself by becoming obedient to the point of death, even death on a cross. Therefore God has highly exalted him and bestowed on him the name that is above every name, so that at the name of Jesus every knee should bow, in heaven and on earth and under the earth, and every tongue confess that Jesus Christ is Lord, to the glory of God the Father.

Reading through that passage might sound like the opposite of having boundaries. Look at how Jesus is described here! Counting others as more significant to himself, looking out for others' interest above his own, emptying himself, becoming a servant, humbling himself, becoming obedient.

Consider, though, the way all of this is phrased: *Have this mind among yourselves, which is yours in Christ Jesus.*

Remember 1 Corinthians 2:16, which tells us that through the Spirit, we have access to the very mind of Christ. Because Christ ransomed us and calls us his own, we can know what he desires from us. And we have an entire Book that outlines what those desires look like.

And guess what that Book tells us?

Christ had boundaries.

He had boundaries on his time—he didn't stay in one place of ministry longer than was best, and he often withdrew to privately pray instead of offering more hours to public ministry. He had boundaries with his abilities—he did not heal every single person he encountered, nor did he always perform signs and wonders when people asked (in fact, sometimes he even rebuked the people asking for such signs). He had boundaries on his allegiance—he wasn't ultimately here for his mother; he was here for his Father in heaven. He even had boundaries on how he allowed others to talk to him—from Satan to a disciple unwittingly sounding a lot like Satan.

Jesus even tells his disciples when to press in and when to shake the dust from their sandals and walk away (Matt. 10:14).

Christ had these boundaries for the very purpose outlined in the last clause of the chapter we just read: "to the glory of God the Father" (Phil. 2:11 ESV).

Boundaries are what enable us to serve God to the utmost of our ability by prioritizing the mission that he's given us on this earth.

When we are being vulnerable about patterns of shame in our lives, we are giving other believers the opportunity to obey God by bearing our burdens with meekness and humility. If they react in any other way, they are giving *us* the opportunity to point them back to God's best for our relationships.

This is not about writing off toxic people. This is about faithfully setting healthy, scriptural lines around how we allow ourselves to be treated. Once we have lovingly communicated these boundaries, the other party is free to set some parameters of their own, and from there, we are able to see if the relationship is capable of being a fruitful one.

The Double-Edged Sword

To fight shame (and really, just to live well), we need community.

My counselor told me as much when I sat in her office to talk to her about my fear of miscarriage. She pointed out all the pain that was festering *behind* my loss, and all the shame I felt at not being able to carry my first baby to term. She pointed out that this shame was just growing bigger and louder and scarier while I nursed it in the darkness of my heart instead of sharing the burden with others.

Going to her was my first step to bringing that darkness into the light.

And, by God's grace—and very slowly but surely—I was able to build a community that is faithful to God's desires for friendships. I was able to find women who surround me with love when I'm crippled by shame. Sometimes, that love looks like pointing out when the shame is stemming from sin and urging me toward repentance and restoration. Sometimes, that love looks like reminding me that needing Jesus to walk with me through the valley of shadows is nothing to be ashamed about. Sometimes, they help me through godly grief. Sometimes, they help me through worldly grief.

Sometimes, I'm able to help them.

As I've walked this journey, I've also run into relationships where I've had to put up a boundary that eventually put an end to a friendship. I've tried to do this, not out of malice or anger, but out of a genuine desire to surround myself with people who point me to Jesus, and not to shame-cycles that take my eyes off him.

How do we know the difference between good community and bad community?

Remember the Holy Spirit. Remember, the Holy Spirit is who unites us to the brethren that we can trust. And remember the Word, where so many mysteries about what God would have from us are laid to rest.

We do not have to fight this battle alone, my friend. There may be some pride to swallow when we think about sharing our shame with others. There may be some fear that stems from genuine hurt that was never allowed to heal. There may be some clumsiness, because we've never really been intimate in this way before.

But love can cover it all.

CHAPTER 10

The Last Memory

It was one of those mornings.

Both my five-year-old and three-year-old have school today, and my husband needed the minivan to cart some gear over to an all-day podcast recording, so that meant packing the entire family (infant included) into the car. I was a little slow on the uptake because my newborn decided to haze me from 3:00 to about 4:30 this morning, and the 7:00 a.m. wake-up call for carpool was rough.

After we dropped the kids off, Phillip remembered something he'd left at home. We swung back by the house, and I ran inside to grab it . . .

And was completely caught off-guard by the hurricane we'd left in our wake this morning. There were dishes all over the place, there was trash littered across the table, there were last night's cast-off pajamas on the floor, and this morning's school time accoutrements on every surface. Hurricane Holmes had landed.

When I got back into the car, I sighed and said, "Our house is disgusting."

And my husband—forever honest and forthright and not one for a subtle signal—didn't even look up from his phone: "Yep."

The familiar feeling started at my temples. My hands tightened. My jaw ticked. My heart felt an uncomfortable squeeze. My mind was prepared with a litany of responses about how most of the mess was his—about how I had been really busy meeting a deadline yesterday and hadn't gotten to put the laundry on—about how he'd been sleeping soundly while I was up with the baby—about how I had fed him and a friend dinner last night after my own long day.

There is a time when I would've said every single thing. Today, though, I knew that I was coming home to write this chapter.

Today, I was extremely cognizant of my proclivity toward shame.

In that three-letter *yep*, I heard, not Phillip's words, but the movie that often plays in my mind. This film stars the perfect version of Jasmine—the one who seamlessly always balances work and life. Her house is clean, her deadlines are met, her children are spotlessly clean and polite, and her husband says things like, "Wow! How do you do it all?"

If the movie were a documentary instead of a fantasy, Jasmine would answer, "I don't do it all. I'm not actually real. I'm the Cool Girl."

In that moment, I was not resting in the truth of God's unreserved love for me. I was trying to rest in my own ability to maintain a clean house and a tight schedule.

Have you ever been there?

Have you ever found yourself running on the hamster wheel of life and finding your worth in how well you're running—or doubting your worth when you trip and fall and the other hamsters trample you while they keep up the pace?

Have you ever heard the echo of your self-shaming in the voice of someone who isn't even aware of how deeply you're struggling?

Have you ever looked to someone else to comfort you when your identity seems shaky, only to realize that all the comfort you could possibly ever need is contained in the truth of God's Word?

Have you ever known that truth in your head, but had trouble feeling that truth in your heart?

It Didn't Used to Be Like This

It didn't used to be like this.

As we all know by now, once upon a time, a man and a woman dwelled in complete and utter security of God's love for them. They had an intimacy with him that was walked out day by day in the paradise that he had provided for them.

Before they took a bite of that fruit, Adam and Eve were strangers to shame. All they knew was the perfect love of their Father in heaven. The fruit brought on the first experience of shame—the first experience of running and hiding behind fig leaves from a God who can see us straight through to the marrow.

Yes, we've learned all about how the story of shame started in Genesis. But want to know something amazing? The story of shame has an ending too—and it's not just on the cross, though Jesus did indeed cancel its power over us over two thousand years ago. The full ending finds itself in the book of Revelation, where we see that the *power* of shame is not only canceled, but every trace of its *presence* in the world around us is canceled too. Revelation reveals the beautiful fact that, someday, shame will be no more. We will one day live in the new earth where we will know nothing of embarrassment or hiding, but only shalom, blessing, and approval.

The first memory of shame was in a marriage, and the last memory we see is another, grander marriage—Jesus and the church. The Bible paints a picture of the two living together forever with no wrinkle, spot, blemish, or hiding necessary. It is a relational haven where shame lives no more, and God has the final word. It is where God forever dwells with his people in perfect relationship. It is where we all will be dressed in brilliant robes of Christ's righteousness, not flimsy fig leaves of our own making. Totally secure in his family and his kingdom. Totally sure we belong.

And in that place, this last memory is not the last at all. It's the first one of a brand-new eternity we will journey through forever.

And let me tell you something about that place, friend: there will be no wonder-women, only blood-bought daughters (and sons) of God enjoying shalom in his presence.

Our days on this earth are a mere rehearsal for that day—where shame has not only ended, but it is a strange and distant memory, if we remember it at all.

The first memory of shame was a garden paradise lost. The last memory will not just be a garden recovered, but a whole new city, where we dwell with our God, clothed in not merely the righteousness we were supposed to have in and of ourselves all those years ago, but the righteousness of God himself, which can never be removed from those he has clothed. In that coming kingdom, the gates are always open, not shut (Rev. 21:25).

Just imagine—a world where you're dressed in such fine and everlasting splendor that you could never be exposed in nakedness again. A gate so open and welcoming, you could never be cast out.

This is your future, friend. And mine. Let's rehearse on this earth day as if that's true, because it is.

The In-Between

It's a beautiful vision, right?

But I know how far away it can feel when we're doing life in between the garden and glory. That "already-and-not-yet" of Jesus having defeated shame once and for all on the cross doesn't always *feel* like it jives with our present reality. And walking in the freedom Jesus has purchased for us can feel like a never-ending cycle of catching the lies we speak to ourselves and shouting them down with the truth.

Guess what?

That's *exactly* what it is.

Paul admonished his listeners:

> Therefore, my dear friends, just as you have always obeyed, so now, not only in my presence but even more in my absence, work out your own salvation with fear and trembling. For it is God who is working in you both to will and to work according to his good purpose. (Phil. 2:12–13)

Paul's hearers have already been saved *to the uttermost* (Heb. 7:25 ESV). Christ's words on the cross were absolutely true: it *is* finished (John 19:30). And because it is *done*, we can trust that the good work Christ began in us, *will* be completed (Phil. 1:6).

I want to return to Philippians, but first, let's look at 2 Thessalonians 2:

But we ought to thank God always for you, brothers and sisters loved by the Lord, because from
the beginning God has chosen you for salvation
through sanctification by the Spirit and through
belief in the truth. He called you to this through
our gospel, so that you may obtain the glory of
our Lord Jesus Christ. So then, brothers and sisters, stand firm and hold to the traditions you
were taught, whether by what we said or what we
wrote. (vv. 13–15)

Here, Paul tells the body of Christ that they have been chosen
for sanctification—the ongoing process that makes us more like
God. Sanctification is that process of our minds being conformed
to Christ (Rom. 12:1–2)—of the Holy Spirit giving us the *very
mind of Christ,* as we talked about in previous chapters. Though
we are saved *instantly,* our growth in grace continues until the day
we die. Part of that growth involves holding firm, even when our
present circumstances and feelings seem to contradict the truth of
our salvation.

Paul continues:

May our Lord Jesus Christ himself and God our
Father, who has loved us and given us eternal
encouragement and good hope by grace, encourage your hearts and strengthen you in every good
work and word. (2 Thess. 2:16–17)

We are not alone in this work. The Spirit is working within
us to accomplish God's will for our growth (2 Cor. 3:18). That
growth involves walking in truth both in our word and deed (Eph.

2:10) *and* in thought. We must believe what God has said about himself—and, by extension, what he has said about us.

We work out our salvation as we remind ourselves of the truth of God's love for us—of the sure calling that he has placed on our lives—of his sufficiency when we falter. We can trust him, because he is at work within us.

What *Does* He Say?

God's words to us through the prophet Isaiah in Isaiah 54 are a promise that we can cling to:

> "Fear not, for you will not be ashamed;
>> be not confounded, for you will not be
>> disgraced;
> for you will forget the shame of your youth,
>> and the reproach of your widowhood you will
>> remember no more.
> For your Maker is your husband,
>> the LORD of hosts is his name;
> and the Holy One of Israel is your Redeemer,
>> the God of the whole earth he is called.
> For the Lord has called you
>> like a wife deserted and grieved in spirit,
> like a wife of youth when she is cast off,
>> says your God.
> For a brief moment I deserted you,
>> but with great compassion I will gather you.
> In overflowing anger for a moment
>> I hid my face from you,

> but with everlasting love I will have compassion
> on you,"
>   says the LORD, your Redeemer. (vv. 4–8 ESV)

Remember in the last chapter, when we talked about trusting our community with our vulnerability, and opening up about our shame? The reason why we should be able to trust brothers and sisters in Christ to steward our shame is because they do so in emulation of their Father in heaven.

He is the God who promises that we will not be disgraced—who promises that the shame of our youth will be *forgotten*.

He is the One who redeems us from the shame that is a result of the fall, and of our own personal sin.

He is the One who has forgiven us through his Son Jesus, who does not hold anything over our heads anymore—and never will.

He is the One who knows our inward parts—because he hand-crafted them (Ps. 139:13–16). There is nothing a fig leaf can hide from his sight, and there is no wall in our hearts high enough to keep him out.

And we don't have to keep him out. Because, even as we are laid completely bare in front of him, he accepts us. Period. Not because of what we have done—not because of what we have not done—not because of who we are—not because of who we are not—but because we are his (Eph. 2:8).

Friend, isn't that what we want? Isn't that what we so earnestly long for?

Or rather, isn't that what we're so often *afraid* to long for, because that hope has been so often disappointed by people who used shame as a weapon, or as a motivation, or as a one-up, or as a stand-in for the freeing truth of the gospel of Christ?

The good news is Christ's trustworthiness is not determined by how well people who claim to know him treat us. Christ's love for us is not determined by whether people who claim him love us well. Christ's acceptance of us isn't measured by the acceptance of human hands that so often fumble the ball.

His Word shows us exactly how he loves. And friends, it's to the uttermost.

He Will Never Cast You Out

As we wrap up this book, I'm going to remind you of lessons learned along the journey of shame's story, and God's greater story, because you need to hear it on repeat, just like I do. So here comes a summary I hope you return to over and over again.

Shame's ghost may still try to haunt us.

Accusers may come and go.

Sometimes, the accuser is the devil—and sometimes, people who ought to know better are letting the devil use them. Sometimes, we ourselves are playing devil's advocate—*literally* advocating for the devil in our thought lives.

There is good news for us here: we don't even have to advocate of ourselves before the Father, let alone the enemy. Christ is our Advocate. He stands in the gap and proclaims truth on our behalf (1 John 2:1).

Sometimes, that shame comes from a person who is purposefully accusing us, trying to use shame to manipulate or control us into doing what they think we should be doing. Sometimes, we live so long under the yoke of that shame that it becomes hard to discern between what that person wants from us and what God wants from us—and we're so confused that when we break free of unhelpful influences, it feels like we're disobeying God.

The good news for us here: certain groups may toss us out of their inner circle once we get a handle on our shame, but God stands ready to welcome us with open arms. It is not glorifying him to substitute shame for conviction—manipulation for wisdom—control for discernment. And he's given us access to the very mind of Christ to help us navigate all of those things (1 Cor. 2:16).

Sometimes, the accusations come from sin. Maybe it lies close at hand for a time, and we do things that fly in the face of our identity as blood-bought children of God. Sometimes, it's hard to come to God and trust him for forgiveness because we are so ashamed of the sin that we have committed—are so ashamed of our bareness before him. And instead of thanking him for the sacrifice of his Son and drawing near to the throne of grace with the boldness of children drawing near to an all-wise Father, we hide.

The good news for us here: God already knows exactly where we are when he calls out to us. He knows we have sinned. He stands, faithfully ready to forgive us (1 John 1:9). He has already forgiven us, because the payment for that sin was already made by his Son Jesus once and for all (1 Pet. 3:18).

Sometimes, the accusation comes from our own sense of failing that has nothing to do with sin. It comes from a version of ourselves that we've concocted in our head, who isn't human. This version has no weaknesses, and never needs to draw near to the throne of grace. This version has no shortcomings, and never needs to repent and correct course. This version is wallowing in self-loathing *should* and not in the truth that springs eternal.

The good news for us here: God does not see us through the lens of what we bring to the table. He doesn't not love us more because we got that promotion, because our house is clean, because our kids are well-behaved, because we don't have to be reminded of his truth, because we can do it all alone. He knows we can't. He knows this to such an extent that one of the persons in the Godhead is literally a *Helper* (John 15:26–27 ESV).

God has brought you near, and he will not drive you away. He has set his love on you, and even when you stumble and fall, he will do the work to convict and restore you, all within the safety of his fatherly care and his family.

The other day, I snapped at my oldest son. I came back and apologized to him later, and he laid his head on my shoulder and said, "It's okay, Mama. I forgive you. I'll always forgive you."

He repeated back the words that I have modeled to him so many times. "Wynn, I forgive you. I will always forgive you." "Wynn, I love you. I will always love you."

He believes them to be true, because the world hasn't tossed him around and made him doubt just yet. My deepest hope for my son is that my unwavering love for him illustrates the unwavering love of the God who will *always* forgive him and who will *always* love him. Who will never cast him out.

Adam and Eve were cast out of the garden—and Jesus was cast in shadow, away from God's presence, so that we could be invited back in. Friends, he has already experienced the pain of isolation and humiliation on our behalf. It is not our portion anymore.

It's not *your* portion anymore.

Say it with me: *he will never cast me out*. Shame will come and call you into hiding. But your Father will always call you back into the light, back into his arms. He has brought you into his family and he will never let you go.

You do not have to run or fret. You do not have to resort to your old fig leaves for covering. You have been richly provided for—a covering of Christ's own righteous record, a godly image you are being formed into, a gospel message that has the power to rescue you, a future that is secure, and all the God-given tools you need to fight the good fight until you reach such a future.

It can be so hard to trust in the "already" when we're dwelling in the "not yet." There are no magical words that will make us believe these gospel truths without ever wavering. But when we find that our feelings have run amuck and have us acting like amnesiacs, the Spirit is there to help us remember, to convict us with good grief, to remind us of the Scriptures, to silence our enemy, and to bind us to our fellow brethren in solidarity. Our feelings do not determine the truth of our status with God; Christ's death and resurrection does.

There is no better news for sinners.

Come out of hiding, friend.

Drop those fig leaves.

Look to all that's yours in Christ.

And rest awhile in the arms of the One who has not only covered all your shame, but will never cast you out.

Notes

1. https://www.merriam-webster.com/dictionary/shame
2. This quote of Sartre was found in Jennifer C. Manion, "The Moral Relevance of Shame," *American Philosophical Quarterly* 39, no. 1 (2002): 73–90, http://www.jstor.org/stable/20010058.
3. https://www.merriam-webster.com/dictionary/guilt
4. Gillian Flynn, *Gone Girl* (2012; repr., New York: Ballantine, 2022), 222.
5. Edward Mote, "My Hope Is Built on Nothing Less" (1834), public domain.
6. Andreas J. Köstenberger, L. Scott Kellum, and Charles L Quarles, *The Cradle, the Cross, and the Crown* (Nashville: B&H Publishing Group, 2016), 616.
7. John Bunyan, *The Pilgrim's Progress*, originally published 1678, http://utc.iath.virginia.edu/christn/chfijba3f.html#:~:text=Thou%20 didst%20faint%20at%20first,and%20lose%20thy%20choice%20 things.
8. Bunyan, *The Pilgrim's Progress*.
9. Bunyan, *The Pilgrim's Progress*.
10. Gregg R. Allison, "What Does 'This Rock' Refer to in Matthew 16:18?" The Gospel Coalition, January 16, 2020, https://www.thegospel coalition.org/article/what-does-this-rock-refer-to-matthew-1618/.

11. Wendy Horger Alsup, *Is the Bible Good for Women? Seeking Clarity and Confidence Through a Jesus-Centered Understanding of Scripture* (New York: The Crown Publishing Group, 2017), 53, Kindle Edition.

12. Alsup, *Is the Bible Good for Women?*, 54.

13. Alsup, *Is the Bible Good for Women?*